Creating a
Data-Informed Culture
in Community Colleges

Creating a Data-Informed Culture in Community Colleges

A NEW MODEL FOR EDUCATORS

Brad C. Phillips
Jordan E. Horowitz

HARVARD EDUCATION PRESS
Cambridge, Massachusetts

Second Printing, 2018

Paperback ISBN 978-1-68253-087-0
Library Edition ISBN 978-1-68253-088-7

Library of Congress Cataloging-in-Publication Data
Names: Phillips, Brad C., author. | Horowitz, Jordan (Jordan E.), author.
Title: Creating a data-informed culture in community colleges : a new model
    for educators / Brad C. Phillips, Jordan E. Horowitz.
Description: Cambridge, Massachusetts : Harvard Education Press, [2017] |
    Includes bibliographical references and index.
Identifiers: LCCN 2017018119| ISBN 9781682530870 (pbk.) |
    ISBN 9781682530887 (library edition)
Subjects: LCSH: Community colleges—United States. | Educational
    accountability—United States. | Education, Higher—United States—
    Evaluation. | Quantitative research.
Classification: LCC LB2328.15.U6 P55 2017 | DDC 378.1/5430973—dc23
LC record available at https://lccn.loc.gov/2017018119

Published by Harvard Education Press,
an imprint of the Harvard Education Publishing Group

Harvard Education Press
8 Story Street
Cambridge, MA 02138

Cover Design: Ciano Design
Cover Image: iStock.com/andresr
The typefaces used in this book are ITC Stone Serif, ITC Stone Sans, and Glober.

To Robert Allen Keith,
professor, mentor, friend

CONTENTS

Introduction   1

PART 1   **A New Model for Data Use**

1. Analytics for Educators   17

2. Human Judgment and Decision Making   35

3. Organizational Habits for Effective Use of Data   51

PART 2 **Putting the Model to Work**

4. Leading and Lagging Indicators   71

5. Aligning Interventions to Indicators of Success   87

6. Monitoring Interventions and Continuous Improvement   107

PART 3 **Case Studies of Data-Use Reforms**

7. Engaging Stakeholders with Data: *Long Beach City College*   123
Lauren Davis Sosenko

8. Data in the Service of Equity: *Southwestern College*   137
Angelica Suarez

9. Leading and Lagging Indicators in Action: *Odessa College*   151
Gregory Williams and Don Wood

Conclusion: *Embracing a New Data Use Paradigm*   173

Notes 181

Acknowledgments 187

About the Authors 189

About the Contributors 191

Index 193

Introduction

Nancy Johnson is a community college president. She considers herself an effective educational leader. Faculty and staff generally like what the college is doing, and the governing board has just renewed her contract. Nevertheless, Nancy believes that the college could be better serving its students and the community. She has a good understanding of its performance based on local, state, and national reports, but when she talks about the data, her words seem to fall on deaf ears. Each month, a new report on some aspect of student success is presented to the governing board, but although the board has made student success a priority, members tend to make only perfunctory comments, often not related to the data presented. Nancy feels there is more that needs to be done to get the message across, but is unsure of what to do to make that happen.

■ ■ ■

Kalib McKenney is a well-respected community college institutional researcher (IR). He has a strong statistics and methodology background, has published an article in an educational research journal, and is considered a seasoned pro by his IR colleagues. Kalib often presents at statewide meetings of IR directors, and attends national conferences in evaluation and institutional research at least once a year. At his own campus, he has created a data warehouse. He uses the latest tools for extracting and reporting information, regularly posting his tables

1

and charts on the IR department website. But the administration and faculty never seem to act on the findings in his reports, and Kalib is frustrated.

■ ■ ■

Denise Spreggs is the English department college chair. She coordinates program review activities and works well with the IR office to gather and share the results of student outcomes, class fill rates, and student satisfaction data. Every five years, a program review is conducted and the data is updated annually. Denise wonders why the faculty in her department are not more engaged in reviewing the data. She feels like it is used more for compliance than provoking the conversations she and her colleagues need to accomplish her department's goals for improving course completion rates, which the English faculty identified as something they want to improve.

■ ■ ■

José Fernandez has just been named Dean of Science and Technology at his college. He recently completed his doctorate in educational administration, and in the program learned a great deal about finance and student outcome data, as well as how to use inquiry as a method for reviewing information. Now he tries to engage both his faculty and fellow deans in discussions about data, but feels that he can only go so far. In the end, his colleagues are less engaged than he would like them to be. He confides to his friends that he believes many faculty and administrators can feel threatened by any discussion about data.

AWASH IN DATA BUT NOT INFORMED

In our over three decades of work with community colleges around the country, we have found that the situations we've just described are typical. Administrators and faculty leaders are struggling with, or at least thinking about, how to better engage their colleagues in discussions using data to improve student success metrics such as course retention, pass rates, persistence, credit accumulation, and completion rates.

Anyone working as an educator in the community colleges knows that they are awash in data. There are national, state, and local accountability metrics; accreditation reports; program review; surveys of students, faculty, staff, and community; and evaluation reports. Yet community college educators struggle to understand and act on available student performance data.

In fall 2014, America's community colleges enrolled 6.7 million of our nation's 17.3 million undergraduate students, many of whom come from low-income households and also are the first generation in their family to go to college.[1] All students are hoping to improve their lives, to earn a living wage, provide for their families, and be productive members of their communities. Unfortunately, many do not achieve their educational goals.[2]

As educators, we want to support student aspirations and do everything we can to help make our students successful. One of the key ways to improve student lives and outcomes is to improve data use. Community college educators need to better understand data, determine what is needed to make improvements in student success, implement those changes, and monitor the impact of those changes. Educators must have data that gets to the point, tells the story, and ultimately informs decisions to act. It must be the right data, in the right hands, at the right time.

Regrettably, the information available to stakeholders falls short in many ways of what is needed to inform decision making and support the changes in policy and practice that will reduce inequities and advance economic opportunities for community college students. Educators are hamstrung because their data use practices are neither effective nor efficient. We have written this book to help.

The purpose of this book is to present a research-based model and an actionable approach to help local community colleges—administrators, researchers, faculty, and staff—to use existing data in ways that lead to improvements in student success. Unlike typical data literacy approaches that put the data at the center of the model, our approach puts the community college educator—the user of the data—at the center. And our model for data use creates a data-informed culture in community colleges. It addresses current efforts to use data in the service of student success by changing data use behaviors.

CURRENT EFFORTS TO USE DATA

Community colleges are at a unique inflection point in their history. Never has there been more attention, more funding opportunities, more initiatives on the national scale, and more opportunity to make improvements in one of our nation's great resources. As educators, we cannot squander this attention.

Funding in many states has increased.[3] But with this new funding comes increased demand for demonstrating success beyond counting the number of students served—and the way to achieve and demonstrate success is to put data to better use. This is not to say that there haven't been, or there are not current, attempts to use data to make improvements in community colleges. A number of initiatives, many on a national scale, are well funded and supported, grounded in the literature, and if executed faithfully, promising.

Achieving the Dream and Completion by Design are good examples of initiatives seeking to improve student outcomes with data supporting the work. Achieving the Dream (AtD) provides a leadership coach and a data coach who, in addition to other supports, help colleges collect and act on data in many areas of student success, beginning with: (1) overall course completion; (2) basic skills course completion; (3) gateway or gatekeeper course completion; (4) persistence fall to spring, fall to fall, and beyond; and (5) completion. That said, as a data coach for AtD, one of Brad's key observations is that the focus on data to date has mostly been about ensuring that institutional research offices have the capacity to gather and report on these and other indicators. It has been focused more on support of changes in policy and practice than on *helping educators use data to inform decision making*. That is now changed with a great step forward with the development of a *Data Discovery Guide*.[4] This new online tool provides many resources to help AtD colleges increase their use of data.

Funded by the Bill and Melinda Gates Foundation, Completion by Design (CBD) provides a framework for colleges to examine and improve their efforts to support students from onboarding through completion, including attainment of degrees, certificates, and transfer to a four-year university. CBD recommends eleven different metrics (key performance indicators, or KPIs). The number of indicators can be overwhelming, and they are not grouped by what metrics are leading and lagging (we'll be discussing this topic in detail in chapter 4). This can overwhelm educators, making it difficult to discern what's actionable or to find the actionable stories in the data.

Two other national initiatives that collect and report data specific to community colleges are the Voluntary Framework of Accountability (VFA) and the National Benchmarking Project (NBP). These initiatives, designed to improve consistency in data collection and reporting and support comparisons between colleges, employ metrics developed by national community college leaders and are collected and reported by participating colleges. While each makes mention of data use, it is assumed that colleges have the capacity to use the agreed-upon metrics on their own to make needed improvements.

In addition to these national initiatives, there are numerous state accountability systems across the United States. One of the most recently inaugurated is in California. This system, known as the Institutional Effectiveness Partnership Initiative (IEPI), is based on indicators in four areas: (1) student performance and outcomes, (2) accreditation status, (3) fiscal health, and (4) programmatic compliance with state and federal guidelines. California's colleges are collecting and reporting data on these sets of accountability indicators.

In most state systems, a majority of the support for developing these is typically on the front end; that is, developing the metrics. Then they expect colleges to supply the information about their student population (or the state system office takes on the task of reporting the information). California colleges that request assistance can receive some help in making use of the indicators. Participating colleges can request volunteers from the field to support their colleagues in this data work.

Beyond the abundance of data reported to national and state systems, almost all colleges also report data on local outcomes. Colleges have developed their own indicators, often generated by the local Institutional Research (IR) office or in some cases, the Information Systems (IS) office. Most often, it is a collaboration between both that produces the numerous reports that get posted to the IR website in the form of fact books or special reports.

FROM DATA TO ACTION

While all of these systems and initiatives provide a great deal of data, they do not in our view focus adequately on the use of data at the local level to inform decision making. We have written this book to close this gap.

We know that engaging in more effective data use practices has the potential to help community college educators improve outcomes because we have seen it happen in our work. The common mantra is that educators want the data they need, when they need it, to make a decision that needs to be made. That said, just having the data is not enough. Having more and better data is not enough. Even having the right data at the right time is not enough.

In this book, we tell the story of how to develop and implement effective data use practices in community colleges. The technical aspects of data use are not central to the process, nor is it more of the same data literacy professional development that others have been promoting. It is not as if there is not enough data in our colleges—there is. It is not as if colleges do not have the right data—they do. And it is not as if community college educators do not have access to the data—while not always easily obtainable, there is accessible data. So if all of the conditions for good data use are in place, why do we argue that it is not enough to be a truly data-informed institution? The quick response is to look at the impact on student success, which has been negligible.[5]

THE SOLUTION: FOCUS ON THE USER AND BEYOND

In thinking about data use and why there seemed to be little improvement in the process (and student outcomes) despite years of effort, we came to an important realization, perhaps owing to our training as psychology clinicians. We realized the focus has been on the data and not on its use. Most attempts to improve data use focus on understanding charts and tables as if these displays would yield actionable knowledge if only we knew how to read them effectively.

We decided to expand this narrow view of data use and go beyond data literacy by adding a considerable focus on analytics (the patterns and other meaningful information gathered from the analysis of data), individual users, and educational organizations. This book is about how educators can make effective use of analytics, increase educator's ability to make judgments about information, use that information to make decisions, and create organizational habits to develop a data-informed institution. We use this research to change the college culture around data use by helping educators to develop analytics, reports, and presentations to fully understand a problem, monitor a practice, and evaluate outcomes—and ultimately, to improve student success.

Community colleges desperately need to improve data use. This book argues for and provides a model and proven practices for doing this. We show how data-use work in the past has ignored the fact that educators have to *make sense* of the data. We show how the way our institutions are structured and the habits of our group behavior inhibit good data use practices and how to change those structures and habits.

We want to be clear: in no way is the intent of this book to "blame the researcher." IR staff do a herculean job of managing the data that they are required to organize and mandated to report. In a typical day, IR staff are extracting data from their student information system (SIS), preparing reports, analyzing survey responses, attending meetings, and more. Their in-boxes are always full; there is always more to do than can be done. They work hard at producing and distributing data.

Unfortunately, with such a load of extremely varied work tasks, with much of the demand coming from a compliance paradigm, they have little time to focus their expertise on data use. So, too often the tables, charts, and reports they generate, or redistribute from federal agencies, state departments, and other entities are in the same format they receive from the source of the information or the local computer programs used to generate the data. And that is just one of the obstacles to putting good data to use.

OBSTACLES TO STRATEGIC DATA USE

As a data coach for Achieving the Dream, Brad was making his first visit to a community college. The research staff was welcoming and cordial, even providing a kolach—a Czech version of pig in a blanket—as a breakfast treat. It was wonderful (and very smart of the IR staff to pro-vide food at a meeting about data—see chapter 2).

The IR staff were orienting Brad to their work, and he noticed a prominently placed award given by a national research organization to the IR department for their fact book. IR was very proud of this achieve-ment. Brad started looking through the fact book, which was displayed in large binders next to the award. It was very comprehensive, comprising hundreds of pages of data. But as Brad studied the large volume, he saw many pages of tables filled with lots of zeroes. Indeed, it would be nearly impossible for anyone to find anything, let alone find any-thing that was useful. Brad pointed this out and asked how the fact book was used by the faculty, staff, and administration. The IR staff did not have an answer to his question—and he was never greeted with a kolach again.

There are a number of obstacles standing in the way of more effec-tive data use. Brad's story illustrates one: the mindset that more data, more tables, more charts, more reports, more sophisticated analysis is better. This approach—what we call the "data jockey" approach—is being rewarded by the institutional research community. But this mind-set, combined with the volume of work that IR professionals confront every day, makes it extremely difficult to focus on a more strategic use of the data.

A second reason is that researchers are trained to produce reports and data displays for publication in journals or presentations at pro-fessional conferences. These reports and displays, however, are not intended to lead to decisions or action. Different users and audiences, those who need to make decisions about policy and practice, require different types of reports and displays.

A third reason that data is not being turned into useful information is because there is a lack of understanding of what it means for data to be actionable. Reporting is driven by stored procedures that make it easy to produce a number of canned reports. It is driven by the accredi-tation, reporting, and compliance needs of the institution; which, in turn, sets up a just-get-it-done mentality. It not driven by the needs of those engaged in improving student success. There are few checks on

the quality of the data by those receiving it, which exace
lem and reinforces this approach. In fact, the Institute fo. ⌐⌐-
ences at the US Department of Education noted, "at least 70 percent and
often 80 to 85 percent of the effort in data analytics is devoted to data
cleaning, formatting, and alignment."[6] When the quality of the data is
poor, how can we expect its use to have an impact?

Even the latest business intelligence software is a culprit. The attrac-
tiveness of these expensive packages is that they can extract and display
data in a multitude of ways. Unfortunately, having more ways to display
data is not necessarily the way to increase data use. The bottom line
is, reports generated by software can obscure the story that educators
need to form a judgment, leading to a decision. Institutional researchers
are using the tools they have at their disposal to fulfill one of their key
functions, compliance reporting, and are overwhelmed with work to
the point that they do not have the time or resources to consider data
use. The effects of this system lead too often to a *Where's Waldo?* game—
a seemingly endless search across reports that look alike and have no
discernable internal pattern or story to tell.

A NEW DATA USE MODEL

The key to our work is to make that data useful, useable, and actionable.
How do we achieve this? According to authors and behavior change
gurus Chip and Dan Heath, there are three important elements needed:
the information has to cause its recipients to *believe* in it, they have to
care about it, and they have to be able to *act* upon that information.[7]
There is little in our current state-of-the-art reporting systems that helps
educators truly engage with data.

Effective data use starts with reframing analytics to make them useful, useable, and actionable, along with an understanding of the research
on how we as human beings engage with data to improve decision making and how we can change organizational habits to improve the use of
data in the service to students.

The model we developed is made up of these three components (see
figure I.1).

FIGURE I.1   The three components of IEBC's data use model

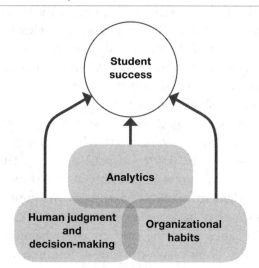

ABOUT THIS BOOK

This book has three parts. Part 1 describes our data-use model in depth and explains how to apply it. In part 2, we map some common student success problems to research-based solutions and discuss how the model can be used for program improvement efforts. Each of the chapters in these sections begins with an illustrative anecdote, many based directly on real-life dilemmas we have encountered in our work with community colleges. Part 3 consists of chapters written by guest authors describing how they have used aspects of the model at their colleges and the results they are seeing. In the final chapter, we bring it all together and explore the future of effective data use.

Part 1: A New Model for Data Use

Chapter 1 addresses the first component of our model: analytics. We open by describing the current state of analytics on college campuses, and tackle the topic of data quality and why it matters. We discuss how analytics can be employed to increase the ability of the user to understand data and dispel six common assumptions about the power of data alone. We also present four rules for effective data use and provide a template for engaging in productive data conversations.

Chapter 2 draws from the latest research about behavioral economics and the role of emotion and the environment to examine the most optimum conditions for considering data. This chapter also addresses how to convey the message through telling the story to ensure all educators clearly understand the data, and provides techniques for clearly communicating the messages that data is purporting to tell. The use of templates for presenting data and for coming to consensus around data is also discussed.

Chapter 3 describes recent organizational theory, including the concept of organizational habits, perhaps most clearly described by Charles Duhigg, whose ideas about habits—how they are built and how they can change—have entered the modern vernacular.[8] Community colleges, like all organizations, have habits that drive a lot of what is done. Using a three-step model for changing habits at the personal level and applying it to organizations, we describe how colleges can examine their habits related to using data, rid their institutions of bad habits, and replace them with effective data use habits.

Part 2: Putting the Model to Work

Chapter 4, introduces the concept of leading and lagging indicators for community colleges and provides examples of their use. Leading and lagging indicators are the vehicle for changing data use in our model. Too often, colleges focus on lagging indicators, which means by the time they get the feedback on their graduation rate, for example, it is too late to take action. Focusing on two or three leading indicators, on the other hand, can be powerful levers for change.

In chapter 5, we describe how our data use model can be employed to successfully address obstacles to student success. This section includes a matrix of high-impact, research-based interventions that can be used to move different indicators of student success, including preparedness, course retention, persistence, basic skill course completion, and college course completion.

Chapter 6 presents a four-stage continuous improvement cycle model and describes how it can be used to monitor and adjust interventions. If leading and lagging indicators are the vehicle for implementing our model, this continuous improvement cycle is the road on which they travel.

Part 3: Case Studies of Data-Driven Reform

In chapter 7, Lauren Davis Sosenko, Director of Institutional Research at Long Beach (California) City College, discusses how a director of institutional research (and former associate director at IEBC) is using the model to improve data use; in particular, how leading and lagging indicators are used to support the college's master plan efforts to improve student success and create a living document.

In chapter 8, Angelica Suarez, Vice President Student Services at Southwestern College (California), describes the how the college applied the model's data use principles to address equity concerns: differential success rates among non-majority subpopulations and special populations (foster youth, veterans, and others). Southwestern College worked with the authors to develop and execute its student equity plan—identifying leading and lagging indicators, implementing research-based interventions, and integrating an evaluation process that helped determine the effectiveness of each intervention. The chapter details the plan, along with the process the college employed and the impact of the work.

In chapter 9, Odessa Community College President Gregory Williams and Vice President for Institutional Effectiveness Don Wood describe how their college's focus on leading indicators transformed the institution into one of the highest-performing two-year colleges in the nation. No other college in the nation has had such rapid and sustained improvement. The chapter authors' relentless focus on leading indicators, while ignoring lagging indicators, changed the culture of the college by identifying these leading indicators for *programs*, *policies*, and *practices*. This resulted in meaningful changes to these "three Ps" and the further use of leading indicators to understand the impact of changes made.

Finally, in the concluding chapter, we bring it all together, painting a picture of what data making itself useful looks like as the norm and all the opportunities this opens to successfully serve students.

■ ■ ■

We wrote this book to be a useful resource for understanding and implementing a data-use model that results in action. Throughout, we keep in mind that college educators are working hard to address student success issues on campus and typically struggle with getting the right data and presenting it in ways that can motivate others to action. We include activities that prompt community college educators to consider the realities of data use at their institution and practical ways to address data use issues that do not deny these realities. We know from the successes we have had with colleges around the country that thoughtful and considerate application of the model will lead to improvements in the indicators of student success that are crucial to improving our education outcomes and, ultimately, the lives of our students.

A New Model for Data Use

ONE

Analytics for Educators

Marsha Chapman directs the institutional research office at her college, which has about fifteen thousand students, is located in a suburban setting, and is considered a "good" community college. Marsha has one research analyst and one part-time administrative aide on her staff. She and her analyst spend much of their time extracting data from the student information system, writing research reports, developing survey items, responding to queries from both internal and outside sources, attending meetings, and updating the research database every semester.

To gather their information, they use the latest tools that enable them to extract data in a more efficient fashion, build tables and charts, and add color and emphasis where they think necessary. They post much of this information on both their internal and external websites in an effort to inform the college faculty and staff, as well as the wider community, about the college's performance. They are tasked with far more than they can possibly accomplish, and at times the work is simply overwhelming.

But although she and her staff circulate so much information so widely, Marsha has no idea how it is used by the college community or viewed by the community at large. She has some sense that the data must be used because college administrators, faculty, and staff frequently request research on a particular interest they have. Unfortunately, Marsha does not have time to fulfill these numerous requests. She also does not have time to write long reports about the research she conducts. Most of her "output" is in the form of tables and charts. In the end, Marsha has no idea if her work is having an effect on improving student outcomes.

■ ■ ■

The good news is that this college is interested in data use; the bad news is that there are many missed opportunities by using what we call the "study everything" approach. As noted by Tris Lumley, "Great organizations . . . are built around great data. Data that [allow] them to understand the needs they address, what activities are likely to best address these needs, what actually happens as a result of these activities, and how to allocate resources and tweak what they do for even greater impact."[1]

There are those who believe that if we just had the right indicator and the right data, educators would be motivated to make the changes in policy and practice that will address their challenges and lead to improved student success. The problem with this paradigm is the belief that data, in and of itself, is enough to change behavior. This thinking does not take into account human nature. According to Heath and Heath, statistics alone are not enough.[2] Numbers, tables, and charts in and of themselves are not enough to inform and influence. Rather, it is the story behind the numbers that has the ability to impact educators.

Relying on data alone to impact community colleges is the *Field of Dreams* approach—faith that if you have enough of the right data, problems will solve themselves but many colleges are signing on. The number of companies touting their latest data visualization software and analytics tools has expanded considerably. However, just because a new software can do something doesn't mean it is the right something, and colleges are learning this hard lesson. We often hear from colleagues whose colleges have purchased these packages, admonitions to be cautious and make sure to keep your receipts in case your college needs to return the purchase.

Let us be clear—we are not saying these tools are bad. What we are saying is that these tools are not the panacea for effective data use. That's because these tools ignore the fact that human beings need to interface with information; just increasing access to information or being able to slice and dice and order data in a variety of ways only gets you part of the way there.

The first step to using data effectively is providing and presenting data in a way that is useful, usable, and actionable. In this chapter, we begin by examining some common assumptions about the power of data as a motivator of change, as well as some current problems with data use that can limit its effectiveness. Finally, we introduce some rules that form the basis of our model for data use.

ASSUMPTIONS ABOUT ANALYTICS

According to dictionary.com, analytics is the patterns and other meaningful information gathered from the analysis of data.[3] There are a number of false assumptions about the power of analytics, as if data itself holds magical influencing powers that will cause people to make changes if only it is presented properly. Below we describe some common false assumptions about the power of data and its use.

Assumption 1: Community college faculty and staff are eager to engage in discussions about student performance. In our experience, the opposite is true—the expression "pulling teeth" comes to mind. We have yet to engage with a community college where the above assumption is true. Human nature causes us to be wary of any discussions that call our work into question. While there are a devoted few who are, in fact, eager to have discussions about student performance, the great majority run away from these discussions as if the announcement of the plague has hit their campus. In fact, at a presentation we were giving at a community college in front of twelve hundred faculty and staff, we were called liars: the data we were presenting from their own IR department painted a particularly bleak picture, and they refused to believe it.

Human beings are wired this way—we are threatened by negative information. Most of us have some familiarity with five stages of grief. First published in 1969, Elizabeth Kübler-Ross's book *On Death and Dying* describes the typical reaction of a person who faces trauma, which she breaks down into five stages.[4] We have discovered that the stages of grief can apply to how educators first view data.

Think about the typical reaction among colleagues at your college when any new piece of data is presented, especially if it reflects unfavorably on student success. We find that educators move through these five stages as they would when facing any traumatic experience. However, unlike a true stage model, we find that educators also move back and forth among the stages, taking one step back for every two forward; and sometimes never reach acceptance.

First comes *denial*, evidenced by comments such as "Where does that data come from?" or "What assumptions did you make?" Next, *anger*; the messenger is challenged. Colleagues may say, "Why are we even looking at this data now?" Once denial and anger are experienced, educators move on to *bargaining*: "If I take the time to review the data and develop a plan for improvement, will that be OK?"

Next comes a sense of *hopelessness*, where a person believes there's nothing that can be done can do to fix the problem. "The high schools are not doing their job" or "Students are unprepared for college work" are typical comments that express educators' sense of powerlessness. *Acceptance*, the final stage, is when we believe the data and want to move forward to make a change.

In our experience, educators do not necessarily go through each stage in a linear fashion and they move back and forth among the stages, which feels like no progress is being made. However, if a college is serious about making changes to policies and practices that improve student success, leadership has to persevere (especially through the anger stage, which can be intimidating), use data appropriately, and help fellow educators work through these stages.

Assumption 2: Just knowing there is a problem is enough to make a change. There is, unfortunately, often disagreement about the extent of the problem a college is trying to address, the degree of influence it has on behavior and doing something about that problem. Consider this example: "In the United States, at any given moment, there are over two million alcohol-impaired drivers on the road."[5] Does this mean we never drive for fear of being killed by an impaired driver? No, we go about our day as usual. Do we join MADD? Maybe, but probably not. This piece of important data does not lead the average person to act.

We have a number of challenges in the community colleges, many of which are not being addressed. Knowing something is not the same as doing something. Just having data does not fix the problem. Knowing the problem exists does not fix the problem.

Assumption 3: We know how to fix a certain type of problem. If we had all the answers, we wouldn't be reading this book. Take the goal of improving basic skills outcomes. Community college educators have tried making basic skills more rigorous, improving staff development for faculty, accelerating coursework, improving placement through multiple measures, implementing co-requisites, and modularizing the curriculum. What's the best practice to use? There is disagreement on this, and we don't have all the answers.

Assumption 4: Administrators, faculty, and staff are willing and eager to make improvements in student success. It's human nature to want to keep things as they are. Our species does not like change. Making change in practice and policy is threatening to the existing college culture. Anyone who has tried to make significant changes in practice, challenging the status quo, can affirm it is not necessarily the changes being suggested that are bad, but rather that these changes—any changes—will upset existing structures.

Because colleges are made of people, not machines, leadership can be timid about rocking the boat for fear that the proposed change could be used against them. Educators have long memories. We have worked with colleges where needed interventions were not made because a staff member recalled a change made thirty years ago that resulted in a poor outcome. In these cases, perfection is the enemy of the good.

Assumption 5: Organizations can change practices and policies when necessary. Changing practices and policies is very difficult to do in the community college environment. It often takes years to phase in any new initiative, and with our current governance structure, achieving consensus is difficult at best and, in our community college environment, nothing moves quickly.

We also note a great lack of knowledge of the decision-making process in community colleges. When we interview committee members who have made a recommendation to change a policy or practice, they often cannot tell us what happens to the recommendation. They have some vague sense that it moves to the leadership level, but either do not know what happens next or if the recommendation for a change is not made, cannot tell you why it was rejected.

Assumption 6: Studying everything leads to better decisions. This assumption stems from the fact that our data systems and new tools enable educators to pull vast amounts of data and determine where challenges exist. However, we believe that less is more and that a community college seeking to make a change cannot and should not look at everything. As the old saying goes, if you try to focus on everything, you focus on nothing. Our experience has taught us that it is important to identify a small set of indicators related to a given student success problem (e.g., course retention, success, persistence, completion). By focusing on a carefully selected set of crucial indicators, a college is better able to drill down and discover a rich set of actionable information.

DATA ACCURACY

In addition to assumptions about people and change, there are assumptions about the data. Perhaps the most widely accepted false assumption is that community college data is accurate. We know this is rarely the case. Two of the most important processes of information gathering— data entry and data reporting—can compromise data accuracy.

Data Entry

In 1998, we began a program linking community colleges in a large database in San Diego, California. This work later became known as the California Partnership for Achieving Student Success (Cal–PASS). By 2012, the system included a few hundred million student records from hundreds of K–12 districts, community colleges, and universities. While the system was groundbreaking, we had a major problem with data quality.

How did we know? In the mid-2000s, we thought it would be a good idea to provide reports back to member institutions. At the suggestion of our advisory committee, we produced and distributed a report for every participating institution on basic student success indicators. We were expecting rave reviews about the usefulness of these reports. We couldn't have been more wrong! Universal feedback pointed out to us that the numbers were wrong. "What did you do to our numbers?" administrators would protest in emails—or worse, unexpected phone calls. We knew data quality was an issue, but we had no idea of the significance of the problem.

For example, one institution sent us data on all students dating back three years. In running initial quality checks on this data, we noted that all students were classified as African American, even though the institution was located in a predominantly white region of the state. We alerted the institution of our findings, and it revised its data over a two-year period. But we reasoned that if the institution got race/ethnicity wrong, there were probably a lot more issues that needed to be addressed in its data.

Data quality is not just an issue in California; it has been an issue in every state where we have worked, and it starts with how data is collected. For example, we discovered that the enrollment application used at one community college district differed depending on the site at which a student enrolled. For example, not only the questions, but the response sets were ordered differently; and for a few of the response sets, the wording was also different. From survey research we know that when response sets are mixed, students will enter information at different rates.[6] No wonder there were discrepancies in the data.

If we expect reports, tables, and charts to be free of errors, the issue of data quality must be addressed. This is not only a community college problem, but one that affects every educational level. In fact, the US Department of Education estimates that "at least 70 percent and often 80 to 85 percent of the effort in data analytics is devoted to data cleaning, formatting, and alignment: the poor quality of education data cannot be ignored."[7]

The truth is, data can be a strategic asset, but not if data quality is suspect. Very few things can be controlled by a community college: buildings are in constant need of unexpected repair, faculty and staff have their own thoughts about the world in which they work, and student behavior cannot be controlled. So what can be controlled? Data.

An institution can control the data that enters its system. But too often, the way data gets into the system and how it is reported (more on this below) is suspect. Even with statewide enrollment systems, there are errors in the data that need to be corrected. Also, one of the dirty little secrets of the data world is that often the categories that need to be reported do not match the categories in the student information system. This means that the IT staffer who must send the data to an external or internal reporting system may have to transform the data to meet reporting standards. And that's a judgment call about how to code the data. No matter how well-intentioned the guess, the end result may be incorrect. To address this, the data that is sent out to both internal and external sources needs to be consistently reviewed. This kind of review is not the norm at our nation's community colleges, but it needs to be if the credibility of reports matters.

Data Reporting

The mountain of data that community colleges receive and produce needs to be transformed into tables, charts, and other displays that help educators understand the meaning behind the numbers. Table 1.1 is a typical example.

Are you able to discern the most important information in this table? Probably not.

This type of presentation, where everything is presented on one page—or worse, multiple pages that look like this table—has little value. Presenting data in this way leaves the user confused and uncertain about what to focus on. It is difficult to identify what is important, let alone have conversations with colleagues about the information and what actions to take, so the presentation actually detracts from data use. It is not that the data is not important, but importance is not enough. The data has to be *helpful* to inform decision making.

As we wrote this chapter, we also accepted an agreement to work with a college to assist with its data use. As part of our process, we have asked for the typical reports that they produced. Being very cooperative, staff sent a series of spreadsheets, tables, and charts that reported on student outcomes—reports typical of what we receive from colleges.

TABLE 1.1   A typical college metrics report

Milestone/momentum point/ on-track indicator	2012	2013	2014	2015	2016
Number of students	3,268	3,237	3,448	3,409	3,588
Completed college math credits in first two years	23%	27%	27%	27%	
Completed college English credits in first two years	50%	53%	53%	57%	
Attempted 12 or more credits in first term	48%	49%	47%	50%	50%
Earned 12 or more credits in first term	26%	24%	26%	27%	28%
Earned general education credits in first term	41%	41%	45%	49%	51%
GPA 2.5 or greater in first term	43%	40%	42%	44%	47%
No withdrawals or failures in first term	47%	42%	45%	45%	48%
No withdrawals or repeats in first year	43%	43%	42%	42%	44%
Earned 12 or more credits in first year (any level)	55%	56%	60%	63%	68%
Earned 12 or more college credits in first year	28%	33%	35%	37%	42%
Earned 30 or more credits in first year (any level)	5%	6%	9%	9%	11%
Earned 30 or more college credits in first year	1%	1%	2%	2%	2%
Earned 20 or more credits in first year	29%	32%	35%	37%	41%
Earned general education credits in first year	61%	61%	65%	69%	73%
GPA of 3.25 or greater in first year	11%	9%	10%	11%	12%
GPA of 2.5 or greater in first year	30%	29%	33%	33%	35%
Earned at least 80% of credits attempted	46%	45%	49%	49%	51%
Pell Award recipient in first year	32%	32%	37%	42%	57%
Retained to second term	72%	74%	76%	79%	82%
Retained to second year	52%	57%	58%	62%	
Enrolled in first summer	31%	34%	36%	37%	44%
Enrolled in second summer	25%	30%	30%	35%	
No delay in enrollment	72%	76%	78%	78%	75%
Underrepresented race or ethnicity	69%	69%	70%	70%	75%
Foreign-born	29%	28%	29%	28%	26%
First generation in college	33%	35%	37%		42%
Average number of terms enrolled in first year	2.0	2.1	2.1	2.2	2.3
Age 25 or older at start	13%	12%	9%	9%	12%
Female	56%	55%	54%	54%	56%
Has enrolled in a fully online course	22%	25%	23%	19%	22%
Three-year success rate	15%	14%	15%		
Six-year success rate	31%				

However, even with our extensive training in research methods and statistics, we did not understand many of their reports. Labels did not make sense and percentages added up to over 100.

The people who had compiled the data were researchers who were well trained and extremely competent about getting data out of the student information system and into the hands of faculty and staff. Unfortunately, if we cannot understand the spreadsheets, neither can faculty or staff who have to make decisions about policy and practice.

This is a case of more is not better—and more complicated is never better. Just because educators can access and report on all of the data does not mean that they should.

PUTTING GOOD DATA-USE PRACTICE TO WORK

To be truly useful, though, data must be more than accurately entered and reported—it needs to be displayed in ways that increase understanding. In this section, we present some practical rules for analytics. We find that when educators follow these rules, they are better able to understand the "story" in the data, and act on it.

Rule 1: Focus

It is said that if a lawyer has ten great points to make, the jury will remember none of them. If the lawyer makes no more than three points, the jury will remember all of the points. This is sage advice. When presenting information, focus on only one to three pieces of data at a time. Any more than that, educators will lose interest. Educators cannot be expected to review multiple pieces of information all at once, form a correct judgment, and act on that information. Again, just because the data can be collected and reported does not mean it is important. Referring back to table 1.1, does it really matter that all of that data is presented? Will a decision on a potential policy or practice change be based on all of those numbers? Although a case can be made for the importance of each piece of data in the table, that does not mean each and every piece of data will be used in a particular decision.

Rule 2: Only Report Data Needed for Compliance or Making a Decision

Big data, the ability to analyze behavior from large data sets, has come to education, and we need to learn how to use it to maximize its value. Just because we have better analytic tools than ever before does not mean that everything big data can do is valuable. One mantra we espouse, beyond reporting for compliance, is: Produce and use data only if it is needed to inform a decision. The implication of this mantra is that data will be produced for two reasons only: to fulfill a compliance mandate or to support decision making.

Rule 3: Use Telling Headlines

We do not often pay attention to the effect a well-crafted headline has on data usefulness. But we should. The power of a good headline is that it describes most of what is needed to know in one simple statement.

Here is an example, using data on chemistry enrollment in a community college. Table 1.2 is a typical table that shows enrollment over time by race/ethnicity and gender.

What is the first thing you notice? We have shown this table numerous times to audiences with hundreds of people. They look at the title and can see trends and difference across the groups and over time, but

TABLE 1.2   Chemistry enrollment data: Typical table

Chemistry enrollment by ethnicity

		Year 1	Year 2	Year 3
African American	Male	15%	17%	16%
	Female	18%	20%	18%
Hispanic	Male	16%	16%	17%
	Female	15%	19%	23%
Caucasian	Male	22%	25%	23%
	Female	20%	19%	19%
Asian	Male	26%	24%	26%
	Female	19%	22%	21%

rarely has an audience member determined the most dramatic change shown by the data. Now, take a look at table 1.3—the same information, with one big difference.

Do you see how the title describes the most important finding? Do you see what your brain does? Your eyes are directed to the line "Hispanic female." And there you can see a radical change: A total of 8 percent more Hispanic females enrolled in chemistry in three years, while every other row is pretty flat.

Not everyone is a data person. So when data is presented, it has to help direct the reader to what is important in the table.

Now, to make it even easier, take a look at the slight format change in table 1.4.

Even better! This tip alone has changed how educators at colleges with whom we have worked understand and make use of their data. Rather than trying to figure out what is important in a piece of data, this reformulation of how data is presented enables educators to focus at once on the "what is important."

Does this mean that only this one line is important? No. Take a look at the table again. It might be possible to highlight instead the differences across racial/ethnic groups or between genders or over time. It depends on what educators care about. The point is, the important

TABLE 1.3   Chemistry enrollment data: Directed title

Hispanic female enrollment in Chemistry increasing

		Year 1	Year 2	Year 3
African American	Male	15%	17%	16%
	Female	18%	20%	18%
Hispanic	Male	16%	16%	17%
	Female	15%	19%	23%
Caucasian	Male	22%	25%	23%
	Female	20%	19%	19%
Asian	Male	26%	24%	26%
	Female	19%	22%	21%

TABLE 1.4   Chemistry enrollment data: Directed title and visual cue

Hispanic female enrollment in Chemistry increasing

		Year 1	Year 2	Year 3
African American	Male	15%	17%	16%
	Female	18%	20%	18%
Hispanic	Male	16%	16%	17%
	Female	15%	19%	23%
Caucasian	Male	22%	25%	23%
	Female	20%	19%	19%
Asian	Male	26%	24%	26%
	Female	19%	22%	21%

statistics need to be prominent and clear if they are to help educators understand an issue and support making a judgment leading to making a decision.

What makes this rule—*Use a headline to highlight what the audience should focus on in any data presentation*—so powerful? Heath and Heath state that statistics are not very helpful in and of themselves. Rather, statistics help us understand a relationship. It is the relationship that has an impact on us and what we remember, not the statistics themselves.[8] In our view, the statistics are really about leading to the conversations that take place about success and change. In order to have a truly informed conversation about student success, the data has to be focused and clear so that it can be easily understood.

Rule 4: Use a Template for Engaging in Data Conversations

Even when data is presented in an appropriate manner, we have observed that educators lack a way to engage thoughtfully with the data. To increase data use, we believe that a series of questions needs to be asked so that everyone understands the information being presented. We have found the following questions to be useful when working with community college educators:

- Is this information accurate?
- What jumps out, and why?
- What are the themes?
- Is comparison data available?
- Does this information challenge current assumptions about this population?
- What might be contributing to their success?
- What might be detracting from their success?
- Is this the data we need to make a decision?
- What is the most important information?
- What is missing?

These questions help to focus a conversation that leads educators to engage with the data, make judgments about it, and decide what to do about an issue of concern.

The first question—*Is this information accurate?*—is an outgrowth of how human beings review any new information. How many times have you looked at a piece of data and simply not believed it was accurate? When data is perceived as inaccurate, everything else is dismissed. This is the first hurdle that any data must clear. If there is any hint that the data is not accurate, the conversation will stop. That is why it is so important to focus on data quality. Furthermore, it is important to describe and defend how the data is defined. For example, how many different definitions are there of a first-time-in-college student (FTIC)? Make sure the categories are clear.

Next, we ask the audience to focus on *What jumps out, and why?* and *What are the themes?* To get a conversation started, educators need to focus on what matters in the data. Everyone in the room must be able to tell the story of what is happening. At this point, before getting to *why* the phenomenon of interest is occurring, it is important to obtain consensus on *what the data is saying*. Too often, educators jump into trying to figure out the why before they have complete information.

We also recommend that it is important to have *comparison information*, either for a different time period, a different demographic group, or even a different but similar institution. Baselines are important; they provide an anchor to gauge our perspective. Educators need to know, for example, if a 67 percent success rate in chemistry is a good success rate.

Educators also need to talk about the underlying assumptions regarding the population under study: *Does this information challenge current assumptions about this population?* Community colleges are striving for all students to reach their goals, but the data shows we do not yet have full equity in our colleges—that some subpopulations tend to do better than others. This does not mean we accept or expect that one population will do better or worse, and there are times that we are pleasantly surprised. The bottom line is we have to be honest and discuss expectations, hopefully with an eye toward achieving equity for all students.

In the majority of the colleges we work with, discussions about data tend to focus on the negative. Too often educators see the weeds first, not the flowers. We suggest you switch from the typical focus on the negative aspects of student performance and start with the positive— the data that shows success. In psychology, there is a principle known as "buildup-breakdown." What this means is that it is best to start therapy with positive information before introducing negative information. When negative information is introduced first, human beings tend to shut down.[9] This applies to educators. We want them to be in a positive mood, have trust in the data, and be confident they will not be blamed for negative outcomes if negative data is introduced.

In the colleges we have worked with, we have found that after less-than-exemplary data is presented, educators work to understand why student performance is poor. Often what happens next is that educators search for reasons for the low performance. Typically, these reasons tend to be focused on the students themselves: students are unprepared, they lack the skills or the prerequisites, they are tired because the class is too early, and so on. In this situation, we refocus the discussion on what can be controlled, rather than on the student as a problem. This is an important shift of perspective. As educators, we have a responsibility to create an environment that maximizes success.

Additionally, we always have to ask ourselves, *Is this the data we need to make a decision? Is there any important data that is missing?* There is a delicate balance between having enough information to make a decision and collecting too much data, which delays any decisions about changes to policy and practice.

COORDINATION OF REPORTING

One last issue on making data credible: Educators have a number of data questions and often do not know whom to ask. So they shoot off an email or make a phone call to their friend in Admissions and Records (A&R) or their colleague in Information Systems (IS). Maybe they have heard that the Institutional Research (IR) office can get the data. Furthermore, their requests are always urgent and they "just need a number" for a grant, the press, program review, whatever. Bottom line: They can't wait. And if their friend in one department is busy, they call another department. Therein lies a problem. Different assumptions and possibly different data sets are used by each department to derive that number, and inevitably, the data will differ across the departments. This affects its credibility.

How does a community college meet the needs of the user and produce data that is not ultimately discounted? We recommended that A&R, IS, and IR come together and decide who provides what data to whom. We know this sounds simplistic, and this is not meant to be obstructionist. But if data is to be credible and to be used, different departments providing data need to come together to make these decisions. We suggest creating a grid that details who does what for whom and when they do so. We have found when this is done, everyone goes away happy.

SUMMARY

This chapter focused on the first component of our model, analytics. There are six false assumptions related to analytics that get in the way of effective data use and that can be resolved using appropriate activities. We cautioned community college educators about the overreliance on big data and the plethora of tools now available to display and manipulate data.

When any data is shared, accuracy is paramount. We presented techniques for maximizing understanding, including focusing on a limited number of key indicators, the use of headlines and highlighting relevant data.

We provided a template for reaching consensus around data and key rules for increasing data use. We closed with a call for collaboration between departments that produce data to community college educators and the public.

Human Judgment and Decision Making

Marissa had just gotten back from her English department meeting at her college. The focus of the meeting was on the recently distributed program review report, which included eighty-nine pages of charts, figures, and tables—some of which had over twenty rows and ten columns. The discussions focused on the number of students who entered basic skills courses in English, did or did not go on to college credit–bearing courses, and students who didn't persist to the following term or academic year. Her colleagues seemed to possess a broad collection of different views on the issues and the solutions. Marissa left the meeting uncomfortably confused and with plenty of questions. Mostly, she wondered how she could use the data to better identify the students who were least likely to be successful in these developmental English courses and what she could do to help them. She also had developed a headache in the warm and overcrowded room; and wondered when she would be able to fit lunch into her busy schedule that day.

■ ■ ■

In this chapter, we present the second component of the data-use model: *human judgment and decision making*. We link the suggestions we made in chapter 1 to what is known about this component—how these suggestions go beyond style and common sense to take advantage of the ways we humans engage with and process information. We also consider elements beyond the simple presentation of information.

A CALL TO JUDGMENT

To successfully use data to improve student success, it is important to acknowledge and understand that the data being provided—data that has been turned into useful, useable, and actionable information—is being consumed by educators. Faculty, administrators, staff, students, the community, and other stakeholders bring their personal histories, training, and perspectives to the way they make sense of information. Part of making sense of data is making judgments about it: its accuracy, its value, and its usefulness. Before decisions can be based on the data, *it has to be judged.*

It is essential to go beyond mere analytics and understand how to capitalize on what is known about how human beings, as sophisticated social animals, process information. It is, of course, impossible to change individual histories, but knowing how people process and make judgments about information—the interplay of personal history, neurobiology, information processing, and the environment—can improve the likelihood that data will be understood and weighed. The judgments people make about something are intimately linked to making decisions. But these two processes do not represent a one-to-one match.

One barrier to making effective judgments and decisions is there often is too much information to process. Below, we explore how information overload presents a significant barrier to processing and judging data, and then follow with ways we can control and shape data that align with human thought processes.

INFORMATION OVERLOAD

The goal of any data display is to improve our ability to make judgments and decisions. A devious enemy of making judgments is that we're often given too much information at once. *Information overload* had been researched for a number of years, but it was in 1970, with Alvin Toffler's book *Future Shock*, that this concept entered the vernacular.[1] Information overload can happen when we are presented with too many charts, tables, and figures in a single report with no clarification or explication. It also can happen when a single table or chart contains too many columns and rows.

To avoid information overload, focusing on the issue at hand is crucial. In the colleges we've worked with, the most progress was made when educators focused on at most three pieces of data. For example, if a college is concerned about course retention, it is essential that this data is not mixed with other indicators such as completion rates and persistence.

One way to avoid too many messages in a single report is to break that report into multiple short documents. Disseminating three short topical reports is more likely to get the impact desired than sending out a single document addressing multiple issues, which may be perceived as unfocused, unwieldy, and overwhelming. Reports that are simple, focused, and easy to understand, with a clear story, are more likely to be read and to lead to educators being able to form a judgment and make a decision.

A good rule of thumb is first to limit the number of displays (figures, charts, tables, diagrams, etc.) to two for each point being made. Using two displays will allow you to make your point visually in two different ways—you can provide information that is easily understood by readers who prefer numbers in tables as well as readers who prefer charts or figures. Figure 2.1 provides an example.

Second, reduce the amount of information in any single display. Consider table 1.1 in chapter 1 again. It's full of columns and rows. It takes an extreme amount of cognitive energy to figure out the story, identify what's important, or tease out relevant data. Too much information in one figure, chart, or table will confuse the audience and make it difficult for them to know what is important.

Unfortunately, many tables and charts have too much going on, even if it is around the same theme. For example, a common report that community colleges produce is a table showing percentages of students in remediation, who go on to college credit–bearing courses, who persist to a certificate or degree, who transfer to a four-year institution, who transfer in the same discipline, and who persist at a four-year institution beyond their first year. These are all important statistics, and with some

FIGURE 2.1   Tailoring information to two types of readers

Table for "number people"

2009 first-year students achieving at
higher rates than 2008 students

Time to degree	2008 first-year students	2009 first-year students
Degree within two years	12%	11%
Degree within four years	31%	42%
Degree within six years	58%	71%

Chart for "picture people"

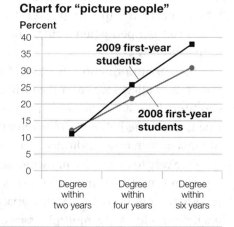

time, educators might be able to discern some patterns. But what issue is this report trying to address? Reducing remediation requires different actionable solutions than increasing transfers to four-year universities. Presenting them all together merely complicates things.

Educators might argue that all of these metrics are essential to track to fully understand what is happening to students. We aren't saying these metrics are not important, do not interact, or are not part of a logic model for student progress and success. We are focused on how to present them in such a way as to maximize judgment and decision making. And to do that successfully, it is imperative that information is simplified in only one display to tell the story.

THE POWER OF TEMPLATES

One of the ways to reduce the likelihood of judgment and decision-making errors due to cognitive strain is with *choice architecture*—the strategic presentation of information in a way that is designed to lead the audience to interpret displays in the way the presenter desires.[2] This is accomplished by "structuring up" the way information is presented in ways that mediate the types of errors people are likely to make.[3]

Think about a report produced at the same time each year about the same topic or indicator. Perhaps it's an annual report on student persistence. If the information is presented the same way in each report, in the same order, with the same heading, it is easier to identify trends and for anomalies to stand out. This also holds true for tables and charts within the report. The same format used for disaggregation by ethnicity should be used for the next table disaggregating by gender, the next table disaggregating by age groups, and so on.

This kind of report that establishes a pattern for presenting information repeatedly and, in that way, capitalizes on people's desire for familiarity, is known as a template. People generally like things that they are accustomed to because these things don't require as much mental work as things that are new and different. Templates provide a natural way to organize information that makes new ideas and data more familiar.

Contrary to what one might think, templates actually increase flexibility.[4] That's because they are easily updateable with new information. Templates also facilitate our ability to see change over time because the information is presented the same way each time. In short, by bringing the same structure to the data every time it is presented, templates allow the audience to focus on content and not on the image in front of them. This, in turn, makes it easier to make a judgment about changes in the indicator and supports decision making.

FOSTERING JUDGMENT BY TELLING A STORY

Another way to aid understanding of data, and thus judgment and decision making, is to tell a story with data. Stories help us connect emotionally as well as cognitively with data, and thus can be a very powerful way of engaging an audience. Well-known evaluator Michael Scriven advises that if you do not have data, then tell a story. If you have data, show the data and focus on the story.[5]

In our culture, stories are familiar ways to communicate information. They have a beginning that sets the context; then a conflict, issue, or problem is introduced; next, the problem is resolved; and finally, consequences follow. This pattern of storytelling also holds for presenting data, and because stories engage us, they can improve judgment and decision making. In table 2.1, we compare a typical fairy tale story pattern with an example of a story about a college.

As the table illustrates, the *context* is set and provides a rationale for action because of the large number of students in this group. The *problem* identifies the less-than-desirable outcome for this subpopulation on the indicator of interest. The *resolution* and *consequences* result from a good understanding of the data and educators collaborating to develop a solution that merits implementation.

The story told with the data must be clear if the audience is to get the message. Sometimes, it is difficult for educators to connect with the data. We use two techniques to address this challenge. First, we turn percentages into numbers. For example, a report may note that 10 percent of the students at a college of ten thousand students have failed to persist. But reporting this as "One thousand students did not achieve their education goals" has greater impact.

The second technique is to put a face on the numbers. We provide pictures of students and describe their lives and struggles and their need to be successful in college to earn a living wage and advance in our society. This has impact because it capitalizes on the emotional reaction of the people in the room.

TABLE 2.1   Using storytelling to present data

Story element	Fairy tale	Your college
Context	Once upon a time, in a land far, far away . . .	Over 40 percent of the population at our institution is under age twenty, and that number is growing.
Problem	There was a young girl who lived in misery with her evil stepmother and stepsisters.	The completion rate for our twenty-and-under students is half of the completion rate for the over-twenty population.
Resolution	She married a prince.	We piloted a support program with peer mentoring for the under-twenties, and their completion rate increased to almost that of the over-twenty student population.
Consequences	She lived happily ever after.	The program is being expanded and institutionalized; and we will continue to monitor impact.

AN ENVIRONMENT FOR POSITIVE DECISION MAKING

The role of emotion has been underutilized in increasing data use. It's hard to avoid the effect of emotion on both judgment and decision making. For hundreds of years, since the Enlightenment, thinkers have hoped that humans are capable of making purely rational decisions. As educators, we want to be rational.

But being purely rational can detract from effective decision making. In fact, it is an impossible challenge. In his 1994 book *Descartes' Error*, neuroscientist Antonio Damasio argues, from a neurobiological stance, that reason and emotions interact to produce our decisions, beliefs, and actions.[6] Damasio maintains that "feelings are a powerful influence on reason, that the brain systems required by the former are enmeshed in those needed by the latter, and that such specific systems are interwoven with those which regulate the body."[7] We cannot separate the feelings that create our experiences from the judgments and decisions we make.

Perhaps the most important aspect of the role of emotions in decision making is that humans are hardwired to process information better—with increased clarity, focus, and mental resources—when we feel safe. As learning environment expert Dan Boudreau notes, there are emotional and physical aspects to the safe learning environment.[8] This means that the internal environment (such as emotion and intellect) can be as important as external factors when we are encouraging judgment and decision making.

It is possible to capitalize on these research findings about environments and learning to increase the likelihood that educators will engage with the data toward successful decision making. We suggest three ways. First, when presenting data create a setting that is comfortable, safe, and familiar. Second, use food to bring people together and to support effective judgment and decision making. And third, implement priming activities to frame and set expectations.

Setting

Imagine sitting in a meeting in a windowless basement room, all the more galling because upstairs the offices have beautiful views outside.

The fluorescent lights are buzzing; the screen for the presentation is not big enough for the projected image, but the projector cannot be moved; the chair arms bang against the tabletops; and the audience cannot orient their seats to face the screen. Physical discomfort translates pretty quickly into negative feelings about the meeting, the presenter—and ultimately, the content.

When planning meetings, there are some important environmental factors to consider. First, ensure that the lighting and air quality are not distracting. Second, make sure the room size and setup meet the needs of those attending and presenting. For example, for small group activities, there should be space for attendees to move around; a large conference table in the middle of the room does not support this kind of interaction. Breaks are often built into the agenda, but some meetings are structured to acknowledge this is a room full of adults, and they can take individual breaks as needed. In this kind of setup, the ways participants take breaks give obvious clues to their comfort level. If they're putting on coats or taking a lot of breaks, these can be signals that the environment is going to interfere with content.

Comfort is only one aspect of the environment to consider. As we mentioned above, for participants to fully engage with the data, they need to feel *safe*. In most cases, physical safety is a given. It's emotional safety that can get in the way of discussions. When the vice president is in the room, can faculty and staff really speak freely or do they politely wait quietly for the vice president's comments?

Having an administrator or supervisor, such as a vice president or dean, in the room can inhibit discussion. We recently held two meetings on a campus. The vice presidents were in the room for the first but not the second. The difference in audience participation was striking. In the first, there was little participation. In the second, we had to cut discussions short so there was time for the next session on the schedule.

Even the presence of administrators who are respected and well-liked by faculty and staff can inhibit the exchange of ideas. More often than not, faculty and staff do not believe they can speak freely in this environment. Preparing campus executives to be absent from a meeting can best support effective data use and decision making, and can ready these executives for anticipated as well as surprising outcomes.

Another block to emotional safety is how disagreements are addressed. Will negative reactions to the data being presented lead to new and innovative action or will the group simply be labeled as naysayers? Kevin Daum identifies ways to respond to those who raise objections to proposed ideas.[9] Some of these responses, in fact, are not designed to overcome naysayers, but rather to recruit them. One way is to give credit to the validity of the objections. Those who have negative views are, after all, helping to identify flaws and obstacles in the group's plans. However, also point out that perfection cannot be the enemy of the good. The goal cannot be to create the *perfect* response to a problem but to create an *excellent* response.[10] Such inclusivity techniques make it safe to speak up in opposition because negative input is respected and transformed into action. An effective response to opposition is one that can be implemented and assessed. It's important to implement this strategy early; to respond to the naysayer by acknowledging the validity of their concerns but not shut down the action agenda.

There also are participants who simply do not feel comfortable speaking up. In our consultation, we recommend a process that creates a safe environment for reacting to data. After the information is presented, everyone in the room writes down his or her response. These are read aloud by one participant, anonymously; and all responses are read before any discussion occurs. Not only does this create a sense of safety, it allows those uncomfortable with speaking in public to collect their thoughts before expressing their opinions.

Food and Information

Another way to create a sense of comfort is to build on the tradition of consumption: real and metaphorical. We have long used food as a way to bring people together. Feeding the group has immediate consequences and implications: a context for sharing is established—sharing information, sharing ideas, and sharing action. The ritual can be as simple as a box of cookies passed among participants or as elaborate as a potluck buffet.

Priming

A third way to put your audience in a state of mind to consume information in a positive manner and to ensure a common starting point is through priming. Priming theory states that images stimulate related thoughts in the minds of audience members.[11] With appropriate priming, the audience for our information is put in a frame of mind to accept and consider the information being presented.

To take advantage of priming techniques, we encourage the use of an opening exercise that puts the audience in a frame of mind to consider the data being presented. For example, we have done a considerable amount of work with California's community colleges' student equity committees; assisting them in using data to inform their decisions about programs, supports, and policies that lead to improved student outcomes on their campuses. We begin every meeting by going around the room and along with name and role, each person states one way he or she has helped a student or group of students toward success in the previous week. This rapid-fire exchange, no more than twenty seconds per person, takes little time and sets the tone for everyone to be thinking about student success, which is the frame for the data being considered. After only a couple of monthly meetings, the group expects the session to begin with these introductions.

Another way we recommend priming the group is to follow the opening introduction exercise with a piece of positive data, such as an increase in course retention rates. The information should be brief, to the point, and immediately evident. Soon, participants begin to expect such information as a standard part of every meeting as well.

Framing Effects

We can improve the likelihood that information will lead to decisions if we frame it properly. Essentially, framing theory states that how we present information can influence how our audience reacts to it. Consider this pair of statements:

A. Our student course success rate is 70 percent.
B. 30 percent of students fail our classes.

You are more likely to feel good about the first example than the second, even though they are the same information. The difference is the way the information is framed.

This framing effect—that logically equivalent statements can produce different results—can be used to increase the likelihood the data we present will lead to action. If there is a problem, frame the data in a way that leads to an emotional response likely to lead to action. Statement B does that. Also note that using the word *fail* sets up priming associations with a negative outcome, which will increase a sense of urgency about the problem.

TO ERR IS HUMAN

Chip and Dan Heath, who have published a number of relevant books about making decisions, facilitating change, and strategies that support successful choices, offer some other decision-making problems we'd like to highlight. The Heaths present four "villains" of decision making—all traps we easily fall into—and detail strategies for defeating them.[12] These four, very human, problems often interact with each other, so solutions to one often can help ameliorate the impact of the others.

Narrow Focus

The first issue to be aware of is that if we see (or think we see) an obvious solution to a problem, we tend to latch on to that solution and look no further. This means we don't explore information that is beyond what we have traditionally examined with similar problems. One way to counteract this tendency to focus on the obvious and visible is to go beyond standard reports and request information that is pertinent to the issue being addressed. For example, be sure the information is disaggregated in ways that directly relate to the questions at hand. Far too often, we go to a college to consult on improving its use of data and we're told, "Our information is not disaggregated in that way." Yet, when we sit down with the IT or IR teams, we find that all they need is the request and they will run the needed reports.

Confirmation Bias

Another barrier to decision making is that people bring their history of beliefs and experiences to the process and accept only information that confirms their beliefs. Or they develop a belief about the problem early in the process, and this limits actions because all they do is explore solutions that are aligned with this belief.

One way to counteract this *confirmation bias* is to gather additional information; in particular, qualitative information. Talk to the students and faculty who deal with the problem term after term, year after year.

Another way to combat confirmation bias is to take time to review information along the way. After a few meetings, it is important to pull those reports out again and review them. Our memories are short for information we don't particularly want to pay attention to. Revisiting information during the decision-making process ensures that pertinent items are not avoided because they don't fit with beliefs established early in the process.

Short-Term Emotional Interference

When we make a difficult decision, our emotions can blind us to available effective options or reinforce our perspective over the perspective of others. For example, long-standing frustrations about dealing with certain groups of underperforming students may begin to diminish the desire to provide assistance. It seems like everything fails, so these students are labeled intractable and the status quo is maintained.

Although it is nearly impossible to remove emotion from the decision-making calculus, it is important to step back and put distance between the emotion and the responses to the problem. Some of the available solutions we already discussed help to suspend short-term emotional interference: bring in other perspectives and revisit the information so facts become more salient.

Overconfidence

The fourth human error that gets in the way of effective decision making is overconfidence. When we spend many years at a college, for instance, we begin to believe in our expertise. We are confident that we've seen it all—we all have the T-shirt. That certainty, however, is merely confirmation of our experiences. We assume we know more than we actually know. We believe we can predict the future based on the past.

Many of the responses already identified can help to address overconfidence issues. Returning to the information can bring back to reality what is known versus what is assumed. Bringing in other perspectives can broaden the sometimes limited information available. Taking time out to reflect can distinguish what is likely from what are magical predictions.

GETTING TO CONSENSUS AND AVOIDING GROUPTHINK

In our consultation with colleges, we frequently encounter individuals who reach different conclusions from the same set of data. This is another reason people don't trust or get discouraged by data: If there were an objective truth to the data, how could so many people come to different interpretations and conclusions? Reaching consensus about what data means can be a frustrating process. But we have a method that can help move your colleagues along.

Before the Meeting

Before data is introduced to any group, we recommend four actions. First, identify the issue to be addressed. Make sure the issue is clear and can be articulated to the group. Second, set the context—why the issue is important and which students are included in the data. Third, clarify the expected outcomes of the discussion. This could include an action solution, further exploration of possible policy and practice interventions, or requests for additional data. Finally, we suggest a bit of advance work checking others' perspectives to better understand how they view the issues.

Introducing the Data During the Meeting

Any data presented during a meeting should guide participants toward a decision. So when introducing data in a meeting, it is important to be prepared. First, know the desired reaction you're hoping for. This will inform how data is presented—as a positive or negative. Second, as we've mentioned many times before, keep it simple. Don't overwhelm the group with too much information. Third, make your data real by turning numbers into faces. Instead of saying that 20 percent of the students are failing to persist to the next term, point out the window and note that if you selected five students walking past the building, one of them will not be here next term. Fourth, engage with the data. The best way to do this is to start with the big picture and then move to specifics. Finally, allow time for discussions among the participants. We've found that the best method is to break the participants up into small groups for a five-minute discussion, then have the groups report out to the whole.

Getting to Consensus

To help your group reach consensus, we created a six-question template to guide discussions—you may remember some of these questions from chapter 1:

- Is this information accurate?
- What jumps out at you, and why (and what are the themes)?
- Does this information challenge current assumptions about this population?
- What might be contributing to success?
- What might be detracting from success?
- Is this the data we need to make a decision about a change in policy or practice (and, if not, what's missing)?

We have found these questions help to clarify the different perspectives of group members. They help the group understand what others think is important, and what they considered in their analysis of the information.

POSTMORTEMS

We are firm believers in meeting postmortems. A final conversation about the meeting and its progress solidifies decisions. These conversations clarify how colleagues feel about the content and process, which goes a long way toward ensuring success of the next meeting and also of any actions the group decides to move on.

Postmortems also help to avoid *groupthink*—when the group avoids raising objections because reaching consensus is a paramount meeting goal.[13] Unlike true consensus, groupthink gets in the way of action. Group members with unspoken concerns raise them later. Interventions do not succeed because the group took too narrow a vision of the issue or did not consider other solutions.

We suggest a postmortem activity that begins by having each person write down a thought or reflection about the meeting. We ask for honest and authentic viewpoints. This is the last opportunity the group members might have to note their concerns. Then we go around the table and have each person state their reflection. Of course, there likely will be duplication. That's okay—what's important is that the meeting ends with everyone feeling heard and, hopefully, all cards on the table.

SUMMARY

In this chapter, we examined human judgment and decision making. Presenting information in ways that reduce cognitive strain while fostering a sense of safety, comfort, and familiarity improves the likelihood that data will be accepted and lead to action. Some key takeaways:

1. Keep presentations simple to increase cognitive ease.
2. Pay attention to your surroundings when presenting data or discussing data reports in a meeting.
3. Feed the group.
4. Enhance a sense of safety by creating a setting that makes it easy for attendees to participate honestly and openly.
5. Frame and present the information in ways that are likely to lead to action.
6. Address the four "villains" of decision making.
7. Data discussions, if they are to lead to action, need to be carefully curated. Introduce data skillfully and ask the right questions to move the group toward consensus. Conduct a postmortem.
8. Above all, remember that making decisions is a human endeavor fraught with the frailties and imperfections of our social and intellectual capacities that can undermine our best intentions. But also remember that with the right presentation, people can be brought to use the data to make effective decisions.

THREE

Organizational Habits for Effective Use of Data

A little girl asks her mom why she cuts the ends off the ham before cooking it. The mother replies, "That's the way my mother always did it. Why don't you call grandma and ask her." So the little girl calls her grandmother, who says, "Well, that's the way my mother always did it. Now your great-grandmother is no longer alive, but her sister—your great-aunt—is. Call her and ask her." So the little girl calls her great-aunt and asks, and her great-aunt says, "Well, my sister never had a roasting dish big enough for the hams she bought, so she cut off the ends to make them fit."

■ ■ ■

According to a Duke University study, roughly 40 percent of our behavior is habit.[1] We do many things in our daily lives without thinking. We brush our teeth the same way. We sleep on the same side of the bed. We put our left shoe on before our right.

Our colleges also are creatures of habit. Community colleges often act a lot like the mom in the Easter ham story. They have been doing the same things—engaging in the same data-related practices, based on the same policies—for as long as staff can remember. Why is that? Because they have always done it that way. Many of these practices and policies no longer make sense. But because they are ingrained habits, they continue despite the fact that they might no longer support educators' needs. In our work with colleges, we find that among all of those reports produced on a regular basis, few—if any—are used by faculty, staff, or administrators. We suggest that it's time to survey the campus community to clarify what information is useful and develop a revised series of reports that meets their needs (instead of ending up unread, on the shelf, or in their email inboxes).

When it comes to data use, we have long-standing habits. We have been producing and consuming data in the same way for quite some time. But how did colleges get here? How did bad habits around data use form? Before we answer that, it helps to understand a bit about habit formation.

UNDERSTANDING HABITS

To better understand habits, how they form, manifest, and can be changed, we turn to Charles Duhigg, an expert on the topic. In his book *The Power of Habit*, he describes an amazing story about toothpaste.[2]

Many of you may be surprised to learn that about the time of World War 1, very few Americans brushed their teeth. In fact, since poor dental health can lead to all sorts of not just dental but medical problems, there was concern that this behavior was creating a national health crisis.

At the same time, the Pepsodent Company of Chicago was trying to sell a new, innovative toothpaste. Despite a great deal of advertising, the product sold poorly. The company tried several strategies to try to increase sales, but none were very effective. One of Pepsodent's investors had a friend, Claude Hopkins, who was considered to be a marketing genius. Using a combination of appeal to vanity and physical prompting, he turned Pepsodent into a household name in less than a decade—and by the end of a decade, about two-thirds of all Americans were brushing their teeth on a regular basis. In fact, more than anyone else, Claude Hopkins can probably be credited for increasing America's dental health. He was able to make these changes because he understood the *habit loop*.

The Habit Loop

A habit begins with a cue (prompt) that signals us. The signal can be visual, audio, or tactile. Next, a routine has to be developed (learned) and as a result of that routine, a reward is obtained. Hopkins created this cue by appealing to our vanity. Pepsodent ran advertisements that talked about that film we all feel on our teeth when we wake up in the morning. The film does not cause dental decay, but the Pepsodent ads implied this, claiming that the product removed the film. They also boasted that Pepsodent whitened teeth—the ads featured a picture of a person with very white teeth and and a glint artfully painted in. The cue (film on teeth), behavior (brushing teeth), and reward (beautiful smile) needed to form habit were all there.

But to lock in that cycle, Pepsodent added an irritant to the toothpaste. This ingredient did nothing to clean teeth, but it locked in a physical feeling, rewarding the user with a tingly sensation. Now, when we think about brushing our teeth, we anticipate the reward—that particular sensation. This anticipation is the motivator to brush.

Habits are powerful and dictate much of our behavior because they create a neurological or psychological craving to do something. They emerge gradually, most of the time without our even knowing; the association with cue and reward is subconscious. So how does all of this research on habit relate to developing good data use habits in the community colleges?

THREE MODELS FOR DATA USE HABITS AT COLLEGES

An effective way to think about habits in community colleges is to relate them to institutional culture. *Merriam-Webster's Dictionary* defines culture as "a way of thinking, behaving, or working that exists in a place or organization such as a business."[3] Every community college has its own unique culture. In order to change institutional culture, we must focus on changing behaviors around data use.

In our work with colleges around the country, we find that data-use habits can be divided into three models that provide us with a starting framework for discussing data culture as habit and lead to our later discussion of how to improve data-use habits. Although we note them as distinct models, they are not mutually exclusive within any one college.

- Model 1: The college does not appreciate data and its uses
- Model 2: The college wants to do something with data but is unsure what to do
- Model 3: The college has embraced the use of data but has yet to realize its potential

Model 1: The College Does Not Appreciate Data and Its Uses

Community colleges following this model have formed a habit of not wanting to deal with data. In some colleges, this attitude arose when data was used to punish faculty and staff, so responses to any report tend to be hostile or defensive. Efforts by the IR staff members (if there are any) to share data widely with faculty and staff tend to be dismissed with comments like, "The data is wrong" and "The data doesn't represent what we do." Any champions of data learn very quickly to not bring attention to themselves for fear of being ostracized by their colleagues.

Leadership also does not value data. Preparing any accountability or oversight data to report to the public or private entities is seen as onerous and taking away from the "real" work of the faculty and staff at the college. The college does not participate in any national or state efforts to collect and report data unless mandated to do so. Even if a college does participate in external efforts, the data is only reviewed for compliance purposes. Planning—which should be data-driven—is done by anecdote, and any data integrated into planning efforts is minimized.

Fortunately, Model 1 colleges are becoming rarer. Part of the reason for this is that as new staff come on board, they are likely to be more savvy consumers of data and have a better understanding of the power of data. They have grown up in the era of technology. Accessing and using data for personal use has become more of a habit to them than it is to long-time faculty and staff members. Unfortunately, educators in this new generation often review data in private, on their own initiative, and use the information to improve their own practice, rather than sharing what they are learning with the senior members of the faculty and staff.

Model 2: The College Wants to Do Something with Data but Is Unsure What to Do

We find most community colleges with whom we work to be Model 2 institutions. These colleges have heard and some know that data and its use are important. They may have a small institutional research office that produces mostly compliance reports and generates some surveys. Once in a while, the IR staff are asked to evaluate a program and program staff do their best to understand and put the results to use. Faculty and staff may understand their own need for data, but it is either hard to obtain, not presented in a way that is actionable, or arrives too late to be useful. They have tried to make sense out of the reports the state generates or from any national efforts in which the college participates, but the information is hard to use and the key stories are confusing.

At Model 2 colleges, there are generally a few data champions trying to get more data from the IR or IT offices, but even they find it difficult to get the information they need in a useful and usable format. These data champions know that if they can just get the right data, they can begin to work on the student success issues that have become more salient in the national education press and more evident at their institution.

Some of these colleges have good data and robust IR and IT offices generating a number of reports. But there is not a critical mass of data users to gain consensus about what it means and how to use it.

Model 3: The College Has Embraced the Use of Data but Has Yet to Realize Its Potential

Model 3 colleges have robust IR and IT offices that regularly produce data, and they often have sophisticated business intelligence tools. The IR function has dedicated websites that include portals through which institutional effectiveness data can be accessed. They produce a large number of reports; some colleges we have worked with provide over two hundred indicators. At Model 3 colleges, some faculty and staff are power data users, engaging with student data at least weekly, and understand how data can help inform their decision making. IR or IT staff have trained key faculty and staff to use fairly complicated systems.

Unfortunately, even Model 3 colleges have data issues, First of all, there is often too much data. The number of indicators is often a source of pride, whether they are being used or not. But as we have noted, just because an indicator can be produced does not mean it is important. Too many indicators create problems about what and how to focus. How does the leadership determine which indicators are the most important? Second, the technology used to produce the data drives too much of what and how the data can and should be produced. This is a case of form over function. Faculty and staff are more excited about the visually stunning tables and charts they can produce than information to be gleaned. A third issue is the expectation that because these tools are available, everyone can be an analyst—all that has to be done is increase access to the data or send more data out for review. The reality is that few educators want to be analysts; they want to be provided with useful information and assisted in applying it toward improving student success. If they do not understand the data, they do not engage in the necessary conversations about addressing issues.

THE EFFECTIVENESS OF ANALYTIC TOOLS

How can colleges change their data-use habits? There are new and better tools that make it easier to analyze, report, and distribute data, so information can be produced in forms that are easier to understand and more useful. But the reality is that the IT and IR offices have been producing and distributing data in the same way since community colleges have been producing data, and just having the new tools is not going to make data more useful.

In fact, in our work with colleges, we have seen that the emergence of these tools has made good data use even more problematic, that their use has actually contributed to bad habits. Four issues in particular have emerged. First, just having access to data and being more able to analyze data has set up a false expectation that the data use problem is solved—that merely providing indicators will lead to engagement. It doesn't. These new and better tools, while creating better access to data, do not help educators better understand the *meaning* behind data. These tools are not analysts.

Second, these sophisticated tools place the development of data in the hands of a select few who know the system. Often, these experts drive the data agenda. But they are programmers, who are trained and think differently than faculty and staff, and they develop the views into the data that they think is best and often in the way they have always done. The data they produce often requires a lot of explaining to its consumers. If data use is to be increased, the process must involve all consumers of data.

Third, because these tools are so robust, the ability to "make indicators" increases. Indicators multiply like rabbits. Even key performance indicators (KPI), which are supposed to be few and specific, can number in the several dozen. For example, we were working with a college recently that has a very talented and technical IR director who developed almost two hundred indicators. When we asked who uses these indictors, the response was, "We don't know, but we want to make these available just in case." But how do community college educators know what to focus on if there are so many metrics potentially to care about? Just because you can generate so much data doesn't mean you should. In fact, we strongly recommend you don't.

Fourth, while the hoped-for result of these tools is to eliminate recursive reports produced by IT and IR, they often do not reduce workload. The idea is that faculty and staff will access indicators via an intranet or online system. However, they do not. Instead, they ask the IR/IT staff for specific information as they need it. This simply adds to the already busy and overloaded schedules IR/IT offices have. Making more work with little evidence of empirical benefit is not helpful. Additionally, many of the reports requested by faculty and staff are ad hoc requests and not programmed into the system, eating up even more time.

Bottom line: While these tools can increase access to data and ease data use, they are not the panacea for good data use habits. They must be created and deployed properly if they are to have a positive impact.

GENERAL RULES FOR HABIT CHANGE

So how do we change a college's data habits to improve use? Let's start with some general habit changes that can support all three models, then we will drill down to specifics.

Before we dive in, it is important to acknowledge that it is difficult, and at times perilous, to attempt to change institutional habits. Remember, a college develops habits over the lifetime of its existence. These habits seem to be locked in. Like all human beings, faculty and staff will be resistant to any change in their habits, especially when this change is not self-motivated. And as noted earlier in this chapter, many administrators and faculty do not attempt to make changes for fear of rocking the boat. Remember the story we told in chapter 1 about one college that was so fearful about making changes that faculty cited examples of the vitriol that was directed at faculty and staff who tried to make a change thirty years earlier!

Never Let a Good Crisis Go to Waste

We find that when there is a crisis—funding, enrollment dropping, a community issue, leadership, a significant mandate from the state, threats from accreditors—it is the best time to introduce new behaviors. This is when maintaining an entrenched culture can take a back seat to survival. This is the time when faculty and staff come together to deal with a threat. Of course, we don't advocate manufacturing a crisis to encourage habit change, but we do advocate taking advantage when one appears.

A crisis helps your community college to focus on a key signature issue. It is a time to change data use habits by acknowledging that the correct information can help to understand the crisis and intervene to address it. Remember the habit loop—the crisis is the prompt. For example, colleges often only look at the big picture, which can mask problems with subpopulations of students or courses. Disaggregating data to identify specifically where the problem is occurring is a habit that often produces a reward by pinpointing the problem. The reward of resolving the crisis is a strong motivator for maintaining newfound habits.

Don't Go It Alone

Data use habits can also be changed by a small and mighty group. There may be a data champion on campus, but it is very difficult for one person alone to change organizational habits. It is important for champions to collaborate to change habits at their college. Often the best team of champions consists of a faculty member and administrator working together. The faculty member represents the practitioners and the administrator represents the bureaucrats. This brings practice and policy into the same change effort by champions who can advocate from both perspectives. Habit change requires a team, even if the team is just two people.

Make Use of the Habit Loop

Duhigg explains that habit change begins with identifying an existing cue, changing the behavior in response to that cue, and the reward.[4] Repetition and reward lock in an effective and appropriate behavior. The first step is to identify existing cues, routines, and rewards.

Let's take the existing activities of a typical community college. All colleges have meetings of standing committees and ad hoc groups to address myriad issues. Meetings are a perfect place to integrate a habit of good data use. Unfortunately, meetings are also a place where good data goes to die. Too often data is presented, but no decisions are made, let alone any analysis conducted. Data is agendized and the committee moves on to the next item, in the interest of time and getting through the agenda. Yet an effective and efficient meeting that uses data for more than *information only* provides an extremely powerful reward, especially when we are used to meetings in which most of the work is expected to be conducted in the gap before the next meeting.

CREATING A NEW HABIT: SUCCESSFULLY INTEGRATING DATA INTO MEETINGS

One of the most powerful ways to change a habit is to develop a template of good practice for how an individual or group is going to act, because a good template describes the desired behavior and supports the behavior with documentation. Using a template also mitigates a typical resistance to change—"We have always done it this way"—by offering the valid response of "We are following the new template."

To help change the habit of data-killing meetings, we recommend using our template for integrating data into meetings. It outlines what needs to be done at three critical stages—before a meeting, before introducing data to the meeting attendees, and while introducing the data and engaging in discussions. Many of the activities and procedures build on what is known about human judgment and decision-making (see chapter 2). Using the template helps the presenter feel better prepared, confident, and comfortable and will help ensure that a team will fully engage around the data. The template is not intended to lead the group to any particular outcome; rather, it puts in place a process to help ensure an actionable outcome will be reached.

TEMPLATE FOR INTRODUCING DATA INTO MEETINGS

Before the Meeting

- **Priming:** Prepare an exercise to start the meeting that puts participants in a state of mind ready to address data. Think back to the discussion of priming in chapter 2. It is important that the priming exercise be very brief, that everyone participates, and, most importantly, that the exercise relates to the data at hand. For example, if the data relates to completion rates, ask committee members to reflect on the feelings they had when they or a family member graduated. This puts members in the mood to focus on success.

- **Framing:** Consider whether to present the data as negative or positive. Too often, data is presented in the negative, which can put educators on the defensive. Think about how these two statements make you feel: "We lost almost a quarter of our first-time college students by the spring semester" and "We were able to retain over three-quarters of our first-time-in-college students in the spring semester." Very different feelings emerge. Framing the data in the negative indicates that it is a big problem. By framing this in the positive it indicates the college is doing pretty well, but still has room to improve.

- **Safety and familiarity:** It is important to ensure that the data presentation will be one where participants feel comfortable and free to provide feedback. Let's return to some of the suggestions in chapter 2. It is important to focus on making sure that all members can speak their minds without threat of retribution. One of the ways to ensure the group feels safe is to have everyone write down their thoughts on the issue being addressed and then read the comments aloud without attribution for discussion. That way, no one knows for sure who said what. Remember, it also provides support to group members who are not comfortable speaking extemporaneously.

- **Meeting arrangements:** Meeting arrangements are too often taken for granted. Make sure that there is food available, as breaking bread together is an important part of our culture that helps a group bond together. Are the tables arranged in a way to facilitate discussion? Are people grouped appropriately? Many colleges hold their meeting in the late afternoon. We strongly suggest a change to this habit—because few people care to deal with data after working all day!

- **Have a detailed agenda:** Does the agenda include what is expected from the data presentation? Any decisions that need to be made should be highlighted. Data should never be presented *for information only*. A detailed agenda lets the participants know what is expected from them up front. By being transparent at the outset of the meeting, there are no comments such as, "I didn't know we were making a decision on this."

- **Clarity of purpose:** When the presenter is prepared, he or she is more likely to have authority and can take advantage of the *halo effect*—that is, by creating an air of authority, the general mood of the meeting will be purposeful as well. Make sure participants know why they are in attendance and the expectations regarding the data. When they know that the data matters and that a decision is expected, they are more likely to move to a decision rather than cogitate about the data.

Before Introducing Data to the Group

- **Identify the issue:** It is important to clearly describe the issue to which the data relates. No matter how clearly the data is presented, there can be misunderstandings. We find it is often highly effective to tell a story as to how the college got to this point and why the data is being presented at this time.

- **Set the context:** Describe the who, what, where, and when the data represents. This is a critical aspect of presenting data. If there are gaps, educators will tend to fill in the blanks. It is important to talk about who is represented by the data; which indicators the data specifically represent and the source; the campus, majors, or classes addressed; and the time period covered. Doing this before disseminating a data display moves the group toward focusing on the content and not on the physical presentation of the data.

- **Clarify the expected outcomes:** Reiterate what decision has to be made. Make sure the group knows what they are expected to do after engaging with the data. It may also be helpful to share the kinds of decisions that could be made using the data. For example, the question could be framed as, "Given this data, we have been asked to consider a recommendation to make a change to practice or policy about . . . "

- **Get participants' perspective:** Participants have expectations and histories that affect how they judge any data presented. Human beings will use their own experiences to justify the why of the data. It is important that these experiences are out in the open in the meeting so that any varying interpretations can be addressed. There is nothing worse than, after a meeting in which data has been discussed, learning that one of the group describes a very different opinion of the data to a person not in attendance.

Introducing the Data and Discussions

- **Consider the hoped-for reaction:** Remember that how the data is framed matters. Is this data meant to increase awareness, ask for help with a problem, evaluate outcomes of a program or service? Framing needs to occur before data is presented. Educators want to be helpful, so if data is framed properly, then the discussion will center around explicit expectations.

- **Keep it simple:** Use only a few displays that highlight only what you want the discussion address. There is a tendency to present all available data about a particular phenomenon of interest. But human beings become overloaded and unsure how to separate the important information from what we call the *noise*. Choose indicators purposefully and resist the temptation to present too much data. There will always be educators who want more information, but the question to ask them is, "If you had this information what might change in terms of your decision making?" Often we have found that when we pose this question, participants will reply, "I just think it would be good to know." *Good to know* is not a good enough reason. *Have to know* is what we are hoping for.

■ **Make it real:** Turn numbers into people—use picture and stories of students as part of the presentation. Remember the student voice. Simple numbers and charts tend to divorce our thinking from the fact that these numbers represent real students. Encourage the group to think about how a 5 percent change in student success means a positive impact on four hundred students on a campus of eight thousand. Ask participants to think about those four hundred students and their families; and how their lives might be changed if the students were successful. Sometimes, before we present any data, we share a picture of one student and we describe her life and the importance of how any changes we make as educators to help her be successful can change her life in a positive way.

■ **Engage with the data:** After describing how a single person is affected, then move on to the big picture with a data display. Too often, data presentations start with the minutiae. Once the big picture is described, move on to any important disaggregation to highlight specific subpopulations or cohorts.

■ **Engage the group:** Make sure to engage in discussions using techniques such as asking participants to write down their conclusions. With large groups (twelve or more), we find it helpful to separate participants into breakout tables to have discussions and then share. Everyone presents before engaging in conversations about options.

■ **Get to consensus on a decision:** Use the data review template as a prompt to ensure the right questions are being asked. This will help the group move toward making a decision.

As this template shows, any presentation of data requires being thoughtful about what is to be accomplished.

REVISITING THE MODELS—HOW TO GET A JUMP START ON INCREASING DATA USE

Now let's turn to some specific solutions for our three models of colleges. Each model has some unique issues that we address with changing habits around data use.

Habit-Changing Strategies for Model 1

Model 1 colleges (the college does not appreciate data and its uses) have an aversion to data. They do not trust it, and actively dismiss it. Let's introduce one way to make the habit change.

First, this college needs a couple of data champions. Remember, one person alone cannot change a habit. It is best if the champions are in leadership roles (faculty or administrator), either formally or informally. Second, the data champions need a place to start the habit change toward organizing around data. One way we do this is for the data champion to ask fellow educators, "Why did you become educators?" When we have engaged in this exercise, we often get a lot of "improve the world" or "improve the community" types of responses. This is the point where data can be introduced to talk about the impact of their efforts. Start with something small and positive, such as the number of students the college has helped achieve their goals (number of completers and successful transfers). Then this data can be introduced and then celebrated—no matter how high or low the number turns out to be—because the goal is to celebrate the use of the data, not the actual outcome.

At this point, educators will begin to ask questions. This is an entry point for changing the habit and when inquiry techniques can be introduced effectively.[5] We find it is important to identify a single, salient topic and utilize inquiry techniques to foster interest in data use. For example, if a college is interested in completion, we find that educators begin to ask questions such as, "What makes our completers different from our non-completers?" At that point, targeted data can be collected and shared to address these questions. The key is to emphasize that the goal is increased understanding, not to judge or blame.

Habit-Changing Strategies for Model 2

We have found that Model 2 colleges (the college wants to do something with data but is unsure what to do) are great to work with. They have the desire to improve data use but have trouble with the specifics. Our concern here is that these colleges may be too eager and want to study everything, turning into a Model 3 college.

To begin with, it is important to use our template for introducing data into meetings (detailed above). Model 2 colleges need structure and technique. Start with a current program, service, or compliance activity (e.g., accreditation, a required state mandate, an external entity that requires data participation). Even though faculty and staff are already willing to increase their data use, it is important to begin with only one or two efforts, and produce data for no more than a handful of related indicators.

Faculty and staff need to review data in their regular meetings. Presenters must have a clear data use strategy. Our coaching encourages Model 2 colleges to develop a process for when and how data is examined; and most importantly, to document what was done with the data and demonstrate how it had an influence on policy and practice.

We encourage data champions at Model 2 colleges to engage with faculty and staff in data efforts that are important to them and where they can easily make a difference. Tackling improving graduation rates may be a heavy lift, but improving student support services and tracking the outcomes of those services is a good start. For example, one college we worked with examined its data and revealed a persistence problem for first-year students. It implemented a robust first-year experience (FYE) program and put mechanisms in place to track those students. Few students volunteered for the FYE, but the data showed that participating students had a 22 percent higher persistence rate (fall to spring semester) than those who did not engage. The college used this information to create mechanisms that increased engagement in the program the next year to over 80 percent of first year students—and that rate continues to increase every year.

The data helped the college justify dedicating resources to a continuing student experience program that focused on keeping students in school. Now, much of its data collection and reporting is on a few student success and persistence indicators. And its data use habits have changed for the better. We helped educators to identify the problem (cue: poor first-year student persistence), engage in a new behavior (routine: targeting the indicators based on an identified issue), and reap the reward (increased student persistence in the first year and on to completion).

Habit-Changing Strategies for Model 3

We have found that Model 3 colleges (the college has embraced the use of data but has yet to realize its potential) can be the most difficult to coach into habit change. Remember, it is very hard to give up something, even if one accepts that less is more. Model 3 colleges typically have fifty-plus indicators (and as noted, we have seen as high as more than two hundred), and they study these incessantly. They also tend to study something to death and then delay action on policy and practice change.

So how does a Model 3 college improve its data use? To begin, it is important to look to the strategic plan. Model 3 colleges typically have too many goals in their strategic plan as well as too much data. Identify one or two goals from the strategic plan that, if accomplished, would make a *significant change in student success*. Collect baseline data on relevant indicators and make sure to disaggregate data by student demographics and other variables. Share the same information in all relevant committees and forums, and push for a decision about changes in policy or practice that would improve the identified goals. Resist the temptation to share any additional data on other indicators.

Once a decision is made, it is important that decision becomes very public. Review and celebrate that a decision has been made and the college is making adjustments in policy and/or implementing a new practice. By focusing on one or two issues, coming to a decision to make changes, and celebrating those changes, the college has now moved from a habit of studying everything to using data to focus on an issue and make improvements.

CREATING GOOD HABITS AROUND ASSESSMENT AND EVALUATION

We have yet to find a college that has good habits around measuring the impact of its efforts. Regardless of their data use model, all colleges need to improve their habits around assessment and evaluation. In fact, we have not seen any college assess more than 10 percent of its initiatives. While the practice is increasing—in part because accreditors are focused more and more on good assessment practices—colleges continue to struggle. To understand the effectiveness of a college's efforts, it is important to make a habit around initiating assessments of student-centered interventions. We address this in more detail in chapter 6, about continuous improvement, but let's start here by examining how a college can make a habit of assessment and evaluation.

One of the ways to initiate good habits of data use for assessment is to ask the following questions each time a new or existing student support initiative is developed or reviewed:

1. How will we know if the (fill in the blank) is improving student outcomes?
2. What students are we hoping will engage in this initiative?
3. What expected outcomes do we think the program will improve?

If you're reviewing an existing program, add the following:

4. Are the students who are participating the ones we hoped would participate?

If your college is serious about monitoring resources and ensuring that they are used in an expeditious and effective way, then these questions will help support good data use habits in achieving those goals.

SUMMARY

Changing habits around data use is hard work, but can be accomplished. Below is a checklist for changing a college's habits around data use.

1. Identify data use habits by looking at the cues, routines, and rewards. What prompts data use? Compliance only or more?

What are the existing routines? Are data discussions something to be dreaded or an opportunity to focus on a shared mission to improving student outcomes?

2. Look for fellow data champions to support increasing data use.

3. Focus on no more than one or two issues to begin data use habit change that encourage educators to focus. Remember, avoid the temptation to use fifty key performance indicators. Limit your focus to one to three.

4. Once a cue has been identified, think about a new routine that can be inserted, such as using the "Template for Introducing Data into Meetings."

5. To increase the utility of data, never provide data for information only. Present it to help inform a decision.

6. Create and widely use templates; they provide an automatic habit change.

PART 2

Putting the Model to Work

FOUR

Leading and Lagging Indicators

One of the rules of driving is that you must obey the speed limit. Now, imagine having to follow the speed limit, but being denied access to a speedometer—only learning how fast you are going after the police officer pulls you over and gives you a ticket. And when you protest, you're told you should have been watching your gas gauge.

■ ■ ■

That's how it is in education. We post the signs for what we want performance to be and publicly report offenders, but do not provide educators with the right gauges for monitoring needs and providing timely responses. Drivers of education need indicators they can respond to in time to make a difference for students.[1]

In this chapter, we introduce and delve into the use of *leading and lagging indicators*. If used properly, they can transform the way a college measures its success. They help to identify beginning and end points. Leading indicators also can support success because they help identify what is in a college's control. And leading indicators provide guidance to understand what is happening along the way, so areas for improvement can be identified while they still can have an impact. Lagging indicators help keep educators' eyes on the prize by identifying the big outcomes typically expected by funders, accreditors, legislators, and other stakeholders.

Leading and lagging indicators provide the information needed to track a college's big goals and engage in formative evaluation along the way that supports student success. Choosing the right indicators also ensures we are working with information that is useful, useable, and actionable.

LEADING AND LAGGING BASICS

The terms *leading* and *lagging indicators* come from the fields of business and economics, which have long used them to predict economic trends. According to Investopedia, "An indicator is anything that can be used to predict future financial or economic trends."[2] We can substitute *student success* or *educational outcomes* for what is being predicted. Our goal in data use is to identify indicators to predict and also indicators that are predictors.

Let's start with definitions, then take a closer look at the differences and what they mean in practical terms for a college.

Lagging Indicators

Lagging indicators are your big goals. They include indicators such as degree and certificate attainment, transfer rates, and job placement rates. Educators tend to focus on them because they are typical accountability measures. These are what the federal government, state higher education system offices, funders, and the public-at-large monitor to determine if a college is succeeding.

But lagging indicators are problematic for a few reasons. They are summative measures with little power to directly influence outcomes. That is, they are tracked for students at the end of their college experience. There is no opportunity to intervene with these students because they are out the door once this information is available. This also means they are not actionable: They do not inform a college when to intervene. They do not identify which students are experiencing difficulties. They do not provide information that allows for identification of research-based solutions to address poor performance. Lagging indicators also only provide information about the survivors.

Lagging indicators are valuable as a beginning point—a benchmark against which progress can be assessed. They are useful for identifying shifts in big outcomes that are generally agreed upon as the metrics of importance.

But the key thing to remember about lagging indicators is they are affected by leading indicators.

Leading Indicators

Leading indicators are directly actionable. This is their defining feature and what sets them apart from lagging indicators. They can be monitored for a student, group of students, or cohort of students. Leading indicators include metrics such as:

- Attendance
- Course pass rates
- Completion of basic skills (remedial/developmental) courses and transitions to college credit-bearing courses
- Term-to-term persistence
- Course grades
- Unit/credit load

Leading indicators directly influence lagging indicators and provide information about student progress on metrics that lead to these big goals. They help to answer questions such as, "What do I need to do well in order to improve my outcome measure or my goal?"[3]

Monitoring leading indicators provides a window of opportunity to act, which ensures that students are on their way to accomplishing the lagging indicators. Students must be progressing or maintaining certain levels on each of these leading indicators to have a positive impact on lagging indicators. Also, if a student or group of students is falling behind, there is an opportunity for faculty and staff to intervene. There are research-based solutions—programs, supports, interventions, and policy changes—that can be implemented to make a difference in the academic success of these students that, in turn, will improve a college's performance on identified lagging indicators.

What Is an Indicator?

Before we get deeper into leading and lagging indicators, it will be helpful to take a look at what is (and is not) an indicator. Indicators are:

- Measurable
- Directly related to student outcomes
- Useful at the group and individual levels

Unfortunately, when we are working with colleges, many of the "indicators" identified in the documents we review—such as action plans, strategic plans, and reports to stakeholders—are not really indicators at all. For instance, we often see items that are focused on faculty or programs and not on students.

Also, a lot of what we see are activities, not indicators; for example:

- All students entering the college will have academic advising.
- The college will provide a first-year experience boot camp in the first ninety days of their freshman year to all students.
- All newly hired faculty will receive professional development about designing student learning outcomes (SLOs) for their courses and be mentored by an experienced faculty member.

These do not inform recipients of what needs to be done at the student level and often are only indirectly related to student success. The second item might seem measurable and student related. But if only 85 percent of freshman students go through the boot camp program, what does that tell you? There is nothing about this item that is actionable other than to get more students into boot camp. To turn this into a leading indicator, the focus would be on a measure of the intended outcomes of the program. For example:

- Ninety-five percent of students attending the first-year experience boot camp will demonstrate the behaviors of students who are successful in college by passing an assessment with a grade of C or better.

Now students who still need supports related to time management, homework expectations, attendance, and other behaviors that lead to student success can be identified. And they can receive those supports, which should address the lagging indicator of increasing persistence.

We also see items that are goals misidentified as indicators. Here are a couple of examples:

- The college will increase the proportion of incoming students who complete remedial/basic skills mathematics and go on to college credit–bearing mathematics in one year by 5 percent per year for the next three years.
- The percentage of students who complete the four-year university general education requirements within three years of enrollment and are transfer-ready will increase by 10 percent in the next four years.

Again, these are not indicators because they do not provide any information related to action that might be taken to improve them. These are program objectives and, at best, lagging indicators.

Note that we're not saying these examples are unimportant or should not be tracked. There needs to be a plan of activities that will address the indicators, and it is important to monitor their implementation. It is important to know how many students are participating to understand those activities' capture rate, because it can be difficult to move the big needle if only a small fraction of the target population is participating in a program.

Most of the colleges we work with have done a fairly good job identifying their lagging indicators—their big goals. But many of the items they identify as indicators (or simply plan to rely on as indicators) are not really indicators at all. We encourage these colleges to rethink their plans and rewrite them as useful tools that can guide their progress along the way. The way to do this is with leading indicators.

How Perspective Complicates Indicators

In this introduction of defining leading and lagging indicators, we have one last item to address. Indicators are not intrinsically leading or lagging. Rather, that is determined by an educator's role or perspective— that is, *whether an indicator is leading or lagging depends on who is using it.* To demonstrate, let's take a look at this indicator:

- Student persistence at a college from the fall semester to spring semester.

For the program staff member who runs a fall freshman experience program, this is a lagging indicator. The program head cannot have any impact on these students because they already are beyond the program's influence. Instead, there might be a leading indicator that can be acted on such as the impact of participation in the program (referred to above). Or, if the students who are not persisting are students who did not go through the program, then an indicator can be created related to increasing participation.

On the other hand, for a dean of student affairs, this is a leading indicator related to the lagging indicator of persistence to degree. The dean can examine the rates of persistence from fall to spring and identify subpopulations of students who need interventions and supports to continue their enrollment. These students are still within the college's circle of influence.

RELATIONSHIPS BETWEEN LEADING AND LAGGING INDICATORS

Now that we've defined leading and lagging indicators, let's turn to how they relate to each other. The first thing to remember is that leading indicators lead to lagging indicators. They are connected by action: acting on leading indicators influences the progress of lagging indicators. Leading and lagging indicators can relate to each other in three distinct ways.

Sequential Leading Indicators

One way leading and lagging indicators can relate to each other is that a set of leading indicators must occur in sequence, one after the other, for students to get to the lagging indicator. Figure 4.1 depicts one such sequence.

In this example, students need to pass basic skills (developmental or remedial) courses before they can move to college credit–bearing courses. These in turn must be passed in order to complete the transfer sequence. Then we can measure our lagging indicator of transfer. We

FIGURE 4.1   Sequential leading indicators: Transfer to four-year institution

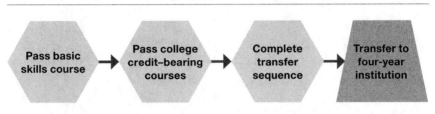

cannot act directly on that lagging indicator. But if students are not achieving the leading indicators, we can identify them at any point in the sequence and intervene with supports.

If there are large groups of students who are not achieving the leading indicators, programs and policies might need to be reviewed. For example, we were working at a college that had extremely low rates of students moving from basic skills courses to college credit–bearing courses. The Basic Skills Coordinator spoke with students and looked at other colleges; and realized that the college's five-semester remedial mathematics sequence was intimidating and discouraging students. We encouraged our clients to imagine being a student who doesn't do well in mathematics and being told he had five semesters of math ahead of him before he could start earning college credit for math courses. The college reworked its program and created an accelerated two-semester remedial math sequence, which increased students' completion rate without compromising the skills they needed in college-level math courses.

Take another measure—graduation rates. Most colleges focus on counting caps and gowns, which has been identified as an inadequate measure of postsecondary institution's performance.[4] Figure 4.2, which seems like a pretty obvious sequence of events, shows why this measure is flawed.

How many of students drop out between their first and second term? How many do not return after their first year? Students must first persist across terms and years before persisting to degrees. And it is these leading indicators that are actionable with research-based solutions.

FIGURE 4.2 Sequential leading indicators: Persistence to second year

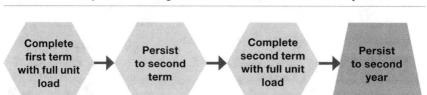

Independent Leading Indicators

Leading indicators also can be independent of each other but together lead to a lagging indicator. Consider the example shown in figure 4.3.

The lagging indicator is degree attainment. There are three leading indicators identified as key for progressing toward the degree. However, none of these is necessarily a precursor to achieving the other two. Although it might negatively impact their education—especially cost—because they are more likely to take courses unrelated to a degree path, students can persist without identifying a program of study. Students

FIGURE 4.3 Independent leading indicators

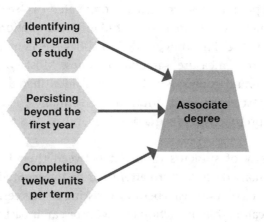

also can persist from term to term without taking a full credit load. However, these are leading indicators that can be monitored to identify students who are less likely to complete a degree.

Combination Relationships Between Leading Indicators

There also can be combination or mixed relationships between leading indicators. That is, some might be sequential and others stand-alone in the lead-up toward their common lagging indicator. Figure 4.4 presents an example of a combination relationship.

In this example, four leading indicators lead to the lagging indicator of degree attainment. The two related to persistence are sequential. Students must persist beyond the first term to persist beyond the first year. However, the other two leading indicators are not necessarily sequential in relation to the persistence indicators or each other.

■ ■ ■

To recap, leading indicators can relate to each other and lead to a common lagging indicator in three ways. They can be sequential, which means that one must happen before the others. They can be independent of each other but lead to a common lagging indicator. Or they can

FIGURE 4.4   Combination of sequential and independent leading indicators

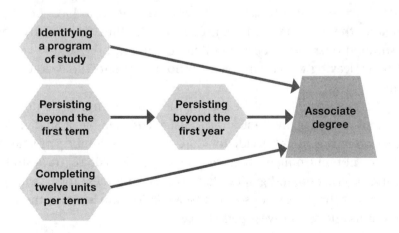

be a combination of the two with some in sequence and others independently connected to a lagging indicator.

It is important to develop a model of indicators and their relationships to each other so it can be determined where to act and for which students. We address this next as we develop some complex—but real—indicator models and explore the necessity of disaggregating a college's data.

A GUIDE TO DEVELOPING INDICATORS

In this section, we examine the process of developing leading and lagging indicators. We'll explore how to select indicators and how to connect leading and lagging indicators, and how many indicators to track.

Select the Right Indicators

Often, we find colleges we work with have a difficult time selecting indicators. On the surface, it seems like an easy procedure, but there are a number of potential pitfalls. A common problem is that the data that will be used to understand what is happening and to develop and implement solutions might not be available at the time it is needed. For example, a college might want to look at enrollment rates in college credit–bearing courses for students who passed basic skills courses the year before. The committee has a meeting in September because they want to be able to intervene early with students who have not registered for the next course in their sequence. But they discover that their institution does not finalize enrollment data until the second week in October, leaving the committee with no data about who is enrolled in which classes.

It also is possible that the leading indicators identified do not actually lead to the lagging indicators at issue. For example, a Student Success Committee might decide to address the high numbers of students who are not returning for their second year and, to do so, track student course completion and grades. But after tracking these for a year, they realize that there does not seem to be a relationship between these two indicators and second-year persistence.

Backward Mapping to Connect Leading and Lagging Indicators

When we work with colleges to identify leading and lagging indicators, we begin with the lagging indicators and *backward map* to the leading indicators. To identify lagging indicators, start with the big goals required to report for funding and accountability. These tend to be generally agreed-upon goals for postsecondary institutions:

- Percentage of first-time-in-college (FTIC) students earning degrees within two, four, and six years of initial enrollment
- Percentage of first-year students returning for a second year (persistence beyond first year)
- Percentage of FTIC students transferring to a four-year postsecondary educational institution within two, four, and six years of initial enrollment

Once lagging indicators have been identified, it's time to think about which leading indicators influence them. Those are the indicators to monitor for action, and it's important to choose the right ones. For each lagging indicator, identify two or three (at most) leading indicators to track. (In chapter 5, we'll present a number of issues and lagging indicators with associated research-based leading indicators.)

Another way to identify leading indicators is to go to the college's program staff. Programs likely are funded because they address issues that are part of a model for improving the institution's big goals. Most colleges have programs to support improvement of basic skills course completion, and many also have a student success initiative aimed at improving persistence among key subpopulations. Objectives from these programs and initiatives can provide obvious leading indicators to monitor.

It is possible that some leading indicators can lead to more than one lagging indicator. It also is possible (and likely) that there will be intermediary lagging indicators. For example, year-to-year persistence can be a lagging indicator, with leading indicators such as course completion rates, attendance, and GPA (see figure 4.5).

But simply because year-to-year persistence must happen before earning a degree doesn't make it a leading indicator. It can be tempting

FIGURE 4.5 Leading indicators with more than one lagging indicator

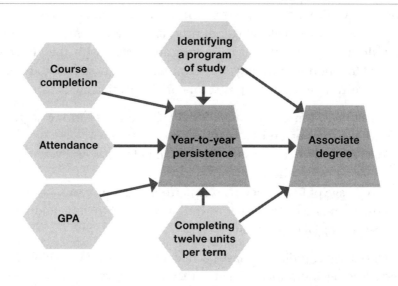

to create complicated models that have many lagging indicators at one point turning into leading indicators at another. But—*and this is crucial*—remember the definitions of leading and lagging indicators:

- Leading indicators are in your control and lead to your hoped-for success.
- Lagging indicators are your big goals and are affected by what you do to influence your leading indicators.

Keeping these in mind will ensure that you avoid turning lagging indicators into leading indicators, because, as we have stressed, lagging indicators are not directly actionable.

The Importance of Disaggregation

Understanding the effectiveness of a college's efforts to help students meet the big goals requires understanding more than simply the influence of leading indicators on lagging indicators. It also requires understanding the performance of subpopulations of students.

To address this issue, it is essential to disaggregate the data. This means examining the progress along leading indicators for subpopulations of students because different programs, services, supports, and policies could affect groups of students in different ways that are systematic. For example, male and female (or other gender identifications) students might experience a STEM summer boot camp differently. Students who receive financial aid might have different experiences with minimum credit loads because of requirements attached to their aid. We encourage exploring differences between demographic subpopulations, students in a program and those who are not receiving those services, full-time and part-time students, students with different academic goals or programs of study, and so on.

Once it is understood how different populations perform on leading indicators, it is possible to design programs, services, supports, and policies that improve the likelihood of each subpopulation's success. It also allows colleges to target certain groups for outreach and marketing about available programs.

COMMON LEADING AND LAGGING INDICATORS FOR COLLEGES

Table 4.1 shows some suggested common leading and lagging indicators. The lagging indicators are drawn from the big goals laid out in publications from funders and policy research organizations such as the American Association of Colleges and Universities and the Bill and Melinda Gates Foundation, or in federal and state legislation. Leading indicators are common metrics available in postsecondary data systems or from simple qualitative data-gathering efforts such as interviews or surveys. In chapter 5, we link indicators to common college student success issues and research-based solutions.

TABLE 4.1   Common lagging indicators and associated leading indicators

Lagging indicators	Leading indicators
Persistence from first year to second year	• Persistence from term to term • Attendance • Grade point average • Course completion rate (grade of C or better)
Persistence to degree	• Identified program of study • Persistence from basic skills to college credit-bearing courses • Persistence from term to term • Terms with full course load • Courses taken outside degree requirements (negatively correlated)
Transfer to four-year postsecondary educational institution	• Identified transfer goal with completion plan • Persistence from basic skills to college credit-bearing courses • Persistence from term to term • Completion of general education and courses in discipline
Cost of degree	• Financial aid package • Identified program of study or transfer goal with completion plan • Persistence from basic skills to college credit-bearing courses • Terms with full course load • Courses taken outside degree requirements (negatively correlated)

SUMMARY

- Leading indicators are in the college's control and lead to hoped-for success. Lagging indicators are the big goals and are affected by what is done to influence the leading indicators.
- Indicators are measurable, directly related to student outcomes, and useful at the group and individual level.

- Whether an indicator is leading or lagging depends on educator role, context, and perspective.
- Leading indicators can relate to lagging indicators as sequential, independent, or mixed.
- When developing an indicator model, keep it simple, start with the lagging indicators and backward map to no more than two or three leading indicators.
- Remember to disaggregate data to identify differential effects on various subpopulations of students.

A Note to Our Research Colleagues

Leading and lagging indicators are similar to regression analyses. Lagging indicators are the dependent variables (DV) and leading indicators are the independent variables (IV). With a multiple regression model, data from a student information system can be used to conduct a path analysis, as well. This could help a college to understand the relative impact of some of the leading indicators on where to focus their efforts and also on the relationships between the leading indicators. By examining the total contribution of leading indicators to the variance in a lagging indicator, colleges can adjust expectations for the likely impact of various efforts.

Student characteristics such as demographics (e.g., ethnicity, gender), status (e.g., financial aid, in basic skills courses), or others (e.g., number of units earned in first term) also could be entered into the model. This information could further assist faculty and program staff in their understanding of how these affect student success and where to focus their efforts.

The leading and lagging model, therefore, can support a variety of interesting analyses that could provide useful information to administrators, faculty, and program staff.

FIVE

Aligning Interventions to Indicators of Success

A community college has been collecting and reporting data on a number of indicators for several years. It now wants to do something about the fact that only 20 percent of all first-time students who enroll in a basic skills class in English or math ever transition to enroll in college-level coursework. For students at one level below college, the transition rate is much higher, about 40 percent, but for those at the lowest level, the transition rate is about 10 percent.

Many of the faculty and staff have floated ideas to address the problem. Recently, a team from the college went to a conference on student success interventions and really liked the first-year experience (FYE) programs. The college held a number of meetings with constituent groups about the idea of implementing a FYE program, and many faculty and staff are ready to roll up their sleeves and get started on implementation planning. They know that designing and implementing a FYE program is daunting and, to do it right, they have to figure out a way to make sure that all first-time-in-college (FTIC) students enter the FYE program, because they learned at the conference that, for an FYE to be successful, most students have to participate.

It takes a full year to plan the effort—select a FYE model to implement, program the student information system to flag the students, publicize the program, train the counselors and FYE faculty, and identity the rooms to ensure they can handle the all of the students participating. Their planning pays off. During the first semester of implementation, over 80 percent of FTIC students enroll in the program. The students report that they like the experience, and despite some challenges, the implementation went fairly smoothly. Everybody is happy.

After two years of implementation, the institutional researcher checks (although nobody has asked her) the levels at which students are entering the basic skills program and how many move on to college-level work. To her dismay, the transition rates from basic skills courses to college-level courses have not changed. She concludes that while the FYE program is going well, it has had no effect on improving basic skills transition rates. The college has chosen the wrong intervention.

■ ■ ■

Hundreds of interventions have been developed and implemented across the nation's community colleges. However, colleges we work with often struggle to identify the one most likely to have an impact on the problem they hope to address. We find that, for example, student supports are implemented when policy changes are needed. Faculty professional development is provided when embedded tutoring is indicated. Or worse, a small, costly, nonscalable intervention is adopted that serves too few students and has no chance of improving identified indicators.

This chapter focuses on the "So what?" question of data use. After all, educators are not reviewing data just to review data. They are working with the data to reveal where action can be taken because they care about their students and their success, improving student's lives, and bettering their community.

THE NEXT BIG STEP: SELECTING INDICATORS

Aligning the problem you are trying to solve with the appropriate intervention answers the "So what?" question. The next step, after selecting the indicators that will lead to success, is to use that data to inform the identification and implementation of policies and programs that have the greatest chance to improve student outcomes. Unfortunately, in our experience, it is not as straightforward a process as it may seem. Colleges are composed of individuals from a variety of backgrounds and with different experiences, as well as needs and wants. In considering any changes, a college cannot divorce itself from the fact any changes that affect students will also affect faculty, staff, and administrators—and, as we have noted in chapter 2, change can be threatening.

We have found that people are more open to change when they can see that changes solve a problem that is holding their students back. We will discuss two critical steps in this process of aligning the intervention to the problem a college is trying to address and how to determine if the high-impact, research-based intervention is the right intervention for the college.

First, we'll present some suggestions on how to determine the problem focus. Then we'll share a way to help ensure that the correct intervention is chosen.

LOOK INWARD

Most colleges have conducted some sort of strategic planning, a process that often includes the college community coming together to determine the direction the college should move; and they usually have a number of planning documents that help guide their actions. These are a good place to start identifying your college's goals. If a strategic planning document is not available or is not specific enough to guide the college, reports gathered from accreditation or state accountability mandates are also a good place to start. Unfortunately, the indicators that accreditors and state accountability measures focus on are lagging indicators. Since by definition, lagging indicators cannot be influenced directly, backward mapping to uncover leading indicators, as described in chapter 4, is the preferred way to begin when using accountability reports. Finally, if a college does not want to start with its strategic planning documents or accountability reports, we suggest that it can begin its data use efforts by looking at just a few indicators.

First, a college should look at its recruitment efforts. After all, there is no other business on the planet that needs to recruit at least 30 percent of new customers every single year to remain viable. Participation rates—that is, the percent of the adult population that attends a college in their region by zip code or by other regional designation—is the data that needs to be gathered. This will give the college a good understanding of who is coming and who is not; and if there are any demographic characteristics that show a gap.

Next, it is a good idea to look at the skill level of entering students. Any assessments that the college uses to determine the level of English, math, and reading proficiency will help the college understand the entering students' preparation level. This data, along with all data we suggest, needs to be disaggregated by demographic characteristics. We also suggest for those students entering right out of high school, an additional breakout be done by high school of origin.

Following the examination of assessment data, it is important to look at the first course students take in their educational career. Research on what is known as *gatekeeper courses* (defined as high-enrollment, low-success-rate courses) shows that this is the point at which many students withdraw or fail and do not return to the institution (and our experience shows that half of these courses will be math-related). Tremendous insight can be gained by looking at the success and withdrawal rates of students in your top ten enrolled courses.

Next we suggest you look at progress metrics, including course retention, course success, and persistence. This is, as we like to say, where the rubber meets the road. Typically, we suggest that colleges focus on two key leading indicators: course retention and course success. If the college's data shows that, on average, course retention is less than 80 percent, this is an area to focus on. If course success rates, on average, show that fewer than 66 percent of enrollments are earning a C grade or better, then it may be a good idea to start here. We have found that if course retention and course success are low, then persistence rates, credit attainment, and graduation rates are likely low as well. Furthermore, these two leading indicators often influence most—if not all—of a college's lagging indicators.

It's also important to look at retention and success rates by individual faculty members. This particular metric is controversial at many colleges, so one way to do this is to examine it in such a way that faculty members do not have to be named in the analysis and can be anonymized. The point of this analysis is to show the range of retention and success rates across a particular course. If course success and retention rates is low, then it's likely the course itself that needs to be examined. If there is considerable variation between instructors, then it is an instructional issue.

Finally, we are increasingly learning that hitting two particular milestones matters for college completion: achieving at least a B course grade, and earning roughly twelve units per semester and twenty-four units per year. Students who do not hit these benchmarks are far less likely to complete than their counterparts.

POLICIES AND PRACTICES ALIGNED WITH STUDENT SUCCESS ISSUES

Let's take a look at table 5.1, which displays some interventions—policies and practices—that have research-based connections to specific problems needed to be addressed at a college. Indicators are listed across the top, with interventions located on the side. This matrix is not intended to be comprehensive, but rather a basic guide to thinking through which policies and practices might fit for the issue a college is working to address.

We used three main sources to compile this matrix, coupled with our experience in working with colleges around the country. The Community College Research Center is the most complete resource.[1] CCRC has reviewed numerous interventions taking place in the nation's community colleges and have detailed information on many of these. The Center for Community College Student Engagement is an excellent source for research as well.[2] While much of the research focused on their survey work, there are excellent publications profiling what colleges have done to address particular problems using targeted interventions. The third resource comes from Achieving the Dream. They have a section called *Interventions Showcase*, and while we would like more evaluation information, the site provides over nine hundred interventions (and growing), and is organized in a very user-friendly manner.[3]

Unfortunately, none of these sources provides information on which intervention to use for what indicator a college is trying to

TABLE 5.1   Matrix of policies and practices linked to success indicators

Indicators of student success

Intervention*	Preparedness	Course retention	Persistence	Basic skills course success	Basic skills sequence success	Course success	Completion
No late registration policy		X				X	
Early warning		X				X	
First -Year Experience program	X		X				
Programs of study (meta majors)			X				X
Completion signaling							X
Summer boot camps				X			
High school–college curriculum alignment	X				X		
PD for faculty on engagement strategies		X		X		X	
PD for faculty on cultural competencies		X		X		X	
Intracollege departmental curriculum alignment	X				X		
Mentoring			X				X
Supplemental instruction		X		X		X	
Course acceleration				X	X		
Appropriate learning outcomes		X					

*Interventions are from Community College Research Center (http://ccrc.tc.columbia.edu/); Center for Community College Student Engagement (http://www.ccsse.org/center/); Achieving the Dream (http://achievingthedream.org/resources/achieving-the-dream-interventions-showcase).

address. Our matrix matches the indicator with the intervention that has been shown to help. But there is more to selecting an intervention than simply matching it to the indicator. Colleges need to ensure that whatever intervention they choose to implement has a good chance of being successful at their institution.

IDENTIFYING AND SELECTING INTERVENTION AT SCALE USING A CRITERIA-SETTING APPROACH

How can a community college determine and select an appropriate intervention that targets the indicator that the college is seeking to improve? We use an overlooked and underutilized exercise to help faculty and staff who are making these determinations. We call this criteria setting.

According to *Merriam-Webster's Dictionary*, a criterion is "a standard on which a judgment or decision may be based."[4] Whenever we work with educators, we encourage them to apply the same standards that they do in their personal life when making large decisions. What do we mean by this? Think about the last major purchase you made, such as a car. When you thought about buying that car, what were your needs? Did you think about safety, two or four doors, reliability, gas mileage, and even the color? These are your criteria. We have noted that the community colleges with which we've worked jump into deciding what intervention to employ without first setting criteria regarding what standards that intervention has to achieve in order to be considered. There are six criteria we bring to the table when making decisions about what interventions to choose:

- The intervention must be able to be *implemented at scale*, meaning that it will serve a great majority of the students experiencing the problem being addressed: no small, nonscalable interventions, or what are often called boutique practices, should be considered.
- The intervention must *align* with the indicator that the college is focusing on, as shown in table 5.1.
- The intervention must be *research-based* and demonstrated to have a *high impact* on the population of interest.

- The intervention must be actually *doable*, and is not some hoped-for effort that has little chance of being implemented faithfully at a college.
- The intervention must be *adequately resourced*. Too often, we have seen colleges begin at a small scale with the hoped-for funding, without considering the scaling effort to come later.
- The intervention must be considered in terms of *systemic effect*. Thinking systemically means considering how this intervention interacts with the other efforts already under way and considering possible downstream effects that could affect other efforts.

Finally a word of advice. In our work, we have noted that modest gains in student success can be made with student service interventions alone. But such efforts, while important, tend to have a limited effect. They simply do not offer enough face time with students, as instruction does. From a time and treatment perspective, students spend the most time in the classroom. Even multiple visits with a counselor, while important, are likely to not have the same impact as a classroom intervention.

Nevertheless, classroom interventions can be harder to argue for than student service interventions. We've found that there is a reticence to implementing instructional interventions because administration doesn't want "to bother the faculty." But the reality is that since students spend most of their time on a college campus in a classroom, the more that we can support faculty in their work, the more likely students will be successful.

The largest gains, however, can be made with a combination of instructional interventions and student services. For example, embedding tutoring in the classroom linked to mentoring provides both a classroom intervention and a staff/student connection. Engagement becomes inescapable for the student.

Moving from Criteria to Intervention

Once criteria have been set, it is time to move forward toward choosing the specific interventions that will align with the college's goals. There are three key steps for doing this:

1. Determine the indicators of interest. For example, do the targeted students exhibit low course retention rates? For those who complete, is the rate of success low (students passing with a C or better, taking the next course in the sequence, etc.)?

2. What are the criteria related to: (a) implementation at scale; (b) alignment between the problem and solution; (c) research-based, high-impact; (d) doable—able to be implemented faithfully; (e) adequate resourcing; and (f) systemically fits with other interventions already under way?

3. Review the intervention matrix, identify potential interventions that meet your criteria and will be accepted by the college community, and explore case studies at colleges that have implemented your short-list of interventions.

Before we leave the setting of criteria, a cautionary note. There are times when colleges have additional resources they can apply to improving student success. Too often, we have seen colleges make these resources available in the form of many small grants to faculty and staff, asking them to think of the next best thing to improve student success. We have never seen any of these small grants go to scale. Furthermore, the grant process itself can cause bad feelings when faculty and departments compete for the funds, and accusations of bias in grant decisions are made. You are far better off using these additional resources to do one big thing rather than thirty small things that affect too few students and show little empirical evidence of changes.

MOVING ON TO INTERVENTIONS

Once criteria have been identified, it is time to consider the interventions that can address the problem you're trying to solve. In this section, we address common student success problems and review the associated high-impact, research-based interventions that have been shown to affect them.

Preparedness

We define *preparedness* as incoming students' readiness to begin college-level work. It also can be defined as students' readiness to move through the curriculum in a sequenced manner. For example, completing a basic skills English course prepares students to succeed in a college-level English course.

If we break down preparedness from the incoming student perspective, we find three situations to address. First, many students, especially those who are first-generation college-goers, do not know how to *do* college. It has been estimated to be between 50 percent and 70 percent of community college-going students in the United States are unprepared for the college experience.[5] They are unaware of the rigors and the expectations college work places on their time and the commitment they need to have to succeed. The research tells us that a first-year experience program (FYE), done well, can help such students understand what is needed to be successful in college. These programs often include information and activities about study skills, time management, and career exploration. The data on FYE programs is quite compelling; they have a proven track record of helping students learn how to do college.[6]

Second, for those students who come to community college unprepared for college work, there is emerging evidence that partnerships between feeder high schools and colleges, which focus on aligning curriculum, have great promise in reducing remediation at the front end. These curriculum alignment partnerships bring faculty—primarily in English and math—together to develop a sequenced and scaffolded set of curricula, with linked student learning outcomes (SLOs), that help to ensure that students are prepared for, and can succeed in, college-level work.

Third, one of the least talked-about issues regarding preparedness is the concern of faculty that many students who engage with and succeed in what would be considered an introductory (100 level) survey course are not successful in the next course in the sequence. This is where internal curriculum alignment, which goes beyond the important work of sequencing and scaffolding that addresses the level of rigor, is crucial.

The key to improving student preparedness here is gaining agreement on the alignment of assignments and assessments—between the high school and the community college faculty, or internally among faculty who teach at the introductory level and above.

Course Retention

Course retention is one of the most underemphasized metrics in community colleges. It is defined as those students who begin a course, stay in class beyond census date, but who end up withdrawing before the class officially ends. And this is one metric that should not be ignored—almost every other success metric we care about relies on ensuring that a student completes a class. This leading indicator is part of a sequenced relationship of leading indicators such as course success, persistence, and unit attainment that leads to lagging indicators such as completion and transfer.

Nationally, we have seen course retention rates as high as 98 percent and as low as 50 percent. Why the disparity? When we explored successful course retention, one of the key factors we discerned is that when students and faculty connect, students stay in class and complete: *Students want to feel cared about.* Think about how simple that can be (e.g., learning and addressing all students by their name shortly after class begins) and the potential magnitude of the impact.

Easy, research-based interventions can support class retention. Professional development can help faculty improve their engagement strategies with students, which helps them feel more connected to one another. It is a basic human tenet that we want to feel connected.[7] The more connected we are, the less likely it is that we will break that tie and, as a result, a student is less likely to withdraw from a class. When we have interviewed students about what motivated them to stay in class (and succeed), many have told us that they did not want to disappoint their instructor.

In student interviews, we also have heard over and over again questions such as: "Why are we learning this material?" and "How is what I am learning going to help me in my career/occupation"? Faculty likely encounter these questions from students as well. So another intervention that holds considerable promise for course retention is ensuring that students understand the relevance of what they are learning; specifically, as it relates to their academic and career goals. If students believe that by dropping the class, they will miss out on things they need to learn, they will likely persist.

Let's operationalize what it means to make the relevance of course material obvious to students. Most importantly, student learning outcomes need to be explicit and understood by students—and those learning outcomes need to be connected to the world of work. Faculty need to engage in developing meaningful and thoughtful student learning outcomes. Unfortunately, developing student learning outcomes is often seen as a compliance effort to support accreditation or other requirements. Faculty need to connect student learning outcomes to the discipline and to the skills and qualifications industry representatives and employers expect. When students better understand the connection the material has to their ultimate goals—to be successful in their career or occupation—it increases course retention rates.[8]

Successful Course Completion

Once a student is retained in class, educators have to work to help students complete the course successfully. *Successful course completion* is typically defined as a student earning a class grade of C or better. A "no late registration" policy has been shown to increase rates of course completion. We find that institutions that allow students to enroll up to two weeks after class begins have very poor course completion rates, and data from the Center for Student Engagement backs this up: students who enroll late (at least one week after class begins) are far less likely to be successful than those who begin class on the first day.[9] Unfortunately, funding pressures related to enrollment lead colleges to continue to implement late enrollment policies. We call this, "Come on in—the door is locked." But if we know that late enrollment policies lead to poor course success rates, then we are committing educational malpractice in order to support the bottom line. And colleges are mistaken in thinking that late enrollment *does* support the bottom line. In fact, the community colleges with whom we have worked that reduced or eliminated late enrollment have not seen a drop in their bottom line (FTE), and students are better prepared to succeed.

Early warning systems have also been used to help students understand how they are faring in class. Unfortunately, we find that electronic early warning systems are not well subscribed to by the faculty, partly because they are not trained on how to use the system. In practice, the best early warning system is strong faculty-student engagement. When, after reviewing an assignment or assessment, an instructor interacts with a student to express concern about the student's performance, it provides an opportunity for the faculty member to help the student learn how to improve. The faculty member then follows up to ensure that the student has followed suggestions to improve course success.

Professional development (PD) for faculty to help them better engage with students, as described above, has also shown to improve course success.[10] This is especially the case with PD specifically in the area of cultural competence. Cultural competence training, which began in medicine years ago, is now beginning to take hold in higher education and is aimed at reducing bias and ensuring fairness in teaching, learning, and assessment. While it is beyond the scope of this chapter to spend a significant amount of time addressing the cultural competence needed to support community college students, evidence suggests that this training helps to reduce barriers to student learning and assessment.[11]

Finally, supplemental instruction—defined as more time on task—has been shown to improve course completion. These interventions include embedded tutoring, after-class tutoring, and practice assessments, among others. Unfortunately many supplemental instruction models are optional, relying on students volunteering to participate, and participation in such models is low. As Kay McClenney, a leading community college advocate, has been known to say, "Students don't do optional."[12]

In fact, it is important to note that any intervention discussed in this chapter should *not* be optional. This holds not only for students but for faculty and staff, as well. If colleges are to make the hoped-for gains in student success, then educators must commit to faithful, full-scale implementation of interventions for all underperforming students. This is not to say interventions should not be piloted. But if, for example, administrators, instructors, and staff believe—and the research shows—that more time on task can improve course success rates, then we need to better integrate supplemental instruction into our courses.

Persistence

We define *persistence* as occurring when a student who begins his or her college career in one term and then continues with education in subsequent terms. We know some states use the term retention to describe this, which can be confusing. But regardless of what your community college calls this phenomenon, it is an important indicator because if students do not persist in their education, they do not complete, and are often left with significant financial debt.

As we noted above, FTIC students often do not have a role model, and so they simply do not know how to do college. FYE programs are becoming a routine part of how community colleges support students entering their institution. We see this in initiatives such as Achieving the Dream and federally funded programs such as those designed to increase minority participation in STEM disciplines. Like any intervention, there are strong and weak FYE programs. The best programs that we have seen engage the students in their very first semester and are not optional. They typically run from eight to sixteen weeks and include three core areas: career exploration, study skills, and time management.

In our experience, the FYE programs that work best are those that require students to enroll if they are taking six or more units or at least half-time enrollment. Also, the best of these programs are taught by both counselors and regular faculty from all disciplines. This model—in which faculty members, regardless of their discipline, can be FYE instructors—is preferred because the techniques instructors learn to deliver in the FYE program are of use in their other classes.

A new set of interventions that have been truly transformative for colleges seeking to improve their persistence and completion rates are *guided pathways*, also known as *pathways of study*, or *meta-majors*. The best description we've found of guided pathways is in *Redesigning America's Community Colleges*, published by the Community College Research Center.[13] In this book, the researchers present compelling reasons why colleges should engage in this transformative work. Specifically, guided pathways succeed because coursework is sequenced and scaffolded to lead students to either transfer to a four-year institution with junior standing in their major or to a degree that prepares them to enter the workforce.

Finally, we know that because many FTIC students are first-generation college students, mentoring programs help them persist in their college work. Such programs, however, are rarely done well because they are difficult to implement and to monitor. That said, when they are done right, they are especially effective for community college students who have not had a role model to help them navigate college. So a faculty, staff member, or experienced student peer who makes an enduring, knowledgeable connection can be vitally important to ensure that students persist from semester to semester and eventually reach their completion goals. We have not seen mentoring programs taken to scale in the colleges that we have visited. However, we believe this is an untapped area that, if implemented rigorously, would lead to educators who reform their thinking: moving beyond teaching and staffing support to building a community college that emphasizes the "community," with students as fully engaged members.

Basic Skill Course Success

Basic skills course success is defined as students who obtain a C or better (or a positive credit) in a course (generally in English, math, reading, or ESL) that is below college level. The data we have seen for basic skills course success is far below the success rate of college-level courses. Think about it: Who are the students in basic skills (or remedial/developmental) courses? Most likely, they have already taken that course in high school or some other postsecondary situation. This means that most of the students in these courses are repeaters; taking the same course they already failed, taught in the same way, and attempting to be successful. This fits neatly into Albert Einstein's definition of insanity—doing something over and over again and expecting a different result.

As an alternative, there is good evidence that students matriculating from high school to the community college who enroll in refresher summer boot camps in English and math tend to raise their placement scores at least one level.[14] These boot camps put students in a very intense, brief experience that seeks to target specific deficits identified by an assessment test. One caveat we have for boot camps is that many colleges will put the student in the program and then retest him or her as a prerequisite to enrolling in the next-level course. We do not agree with this practice. If the faculty member teaching the course believes that the student is prepared to move on, that student should simply be placed in the next-level course. We like to say, "Tests are a proxy for trust." If we trust the instructor to judge that the student has met the appropriate skill level, why are we testing again?

Course acceleration is also an intervention that appears to be improving student success and is being implemented in community colleges across the nation.[15] Specifically, programs such as Mathway, Quantway, and Statway (for mathematics), and the California Acceleration Project (for English) have good positive outcomes for helping students pass out of basic skills courses and into college credit–level courses.[16] Unfortunately, we have noticed that many of these programs are not ubiquitous in basic skills English and mathematics courses. Many colleges have only a few sections dedicated to these accelerated, innovative ways to teach math and English. We have encountered resistance—in some cases, a great deal of resistance—to implementing acceleration in community colleges because it is unfamiliar. While we understand it is difficult to change the way math and English have been taught, it is important for colleges to adopt these proven approaches at scale.

Closely allied with basic skills course success is *basic skills sequence success*; that is, a student enrolling in any level of basic skills and moving through the sequence of courses to achieve a passing grade in a college-level course in the same discipline. It is not unusual for us to encounter extremely low sequence success rates—in some colleges, the percentage of students who start in a low-level basic skills course and move on to succeed in a college-level course is less than 10 percent. A colleague of ours, Rob Johnstone, has stated, "Most students have a greater chance of crossing a moat filled with alligators than they do of moving from a low-level basic skills course to college-level coursework." This is especially true in math.[17]

We encourage you to examine your basic skills sequence and explore how it might be shortened. Can you think of anyone who would endure five terms of courses through which they must struggle to finally get to a college-level course? Yet, we encounter these extremely long sequences around the country.

An emerging effort to improve basic skills sequence success is *basic skills corequisite remediation*. While there are different forms of this approach, it means a basic skills course is paired with a college-level course and the student completes both in one year. This approach minimizes the time to exit out of basic skills coursework and has the added benefit of better aligning learning outcomes from basic skills to college-level coursework.

Finally, it has been our experience that increased faculty engagement, training in cultural competence, and providing supplemental instruction experiences for students also help to support improvements in basic skills course and sequence success.

College Completion

College completion is when a student achieves a degree or certificate, or transfers to a four-year university. The reality is that there are very few direct ways to improve completion—after all, it is the primary lagging indicator in the community colleges. That said, guided pathways, pathways of study, and meta-majors do have a significant impact on improving graduation.[18] Mentoring has the potential to improve completion as well.[19]

Another practice, completion signaling systems, can dramatically improve completion. Completion signaling systems support student success by helping students better understand their own academic progress and how close they are to achieving their goals. Yet very few community colleges are implementing these systems and students rarely know their status. What if there were a system that would let students know how close they are to completion? At the end of every semester a student would receive a communication that gives them this information. This would enable students to make informed decisions about the courses to take and what they need to do to complete.

■ ■ ■

In our work with community colleges, we have seen research-based, high-impact strategies described above successfully taken to scale. These are aligned with the indicators that colleges are trying to address. Note, however, that not all of these strategies will fit well with every college's culture, so when colleges investigate them, we suggest taking steps to ensure that they can be accepted by the college community and implemented faithfully. We close with some suggestions for overcoming resistance.

GETTING TO YES, OR OVERCOMING RESISTANCE IN THE COMMUNITY COLLEGE

We all agree that change is hard in community colleges. In fact, as we have noted, the research tells us that human beings, in general, prefer stasis. People fear the unknown. So how can your college, after identifying an appropriate intervention to implement, ensure buy-in so that intervention will be accepted and move forward?

We suggest that educators look to a change management strategy in order to move forward with any large-scale systemic change in policy, practice, or instruction. The work of John Kotter at Harvard Business School provides a clear understanding of how to do this.[20] We believe that Kotter's work is particularly applicable in community colleges. So let's examine how it can help support implementation of changes to improve student success.

Dealing with resistance is the key issue that needs to be addressed when any change is considered. Resistance can take many forms. But we find that in community colleges, it often comes in the form of our fellow educators claiming that any changes will be too expensive, will not produce the kinds of results that we care about, will not fully address the problems we are trying to solve, and—because the intervention was borrowed from somewhere else and it wasn't created internally—it is looked upon with suspicion and doubt. Furthermore, considering and implementing any change has to go through a Byzantine bureaucracy and community college politics that often are a result of poor trust between administrators and faculty and staff, an aversion to teamwork, and less-than-ideal leadership and management.

Kotter describes an eight-stage process for creating major change. This process begins with helping to create and focus on a *sense of urgency*. Next, a *coalition of leaders* needs to come together to examine the problem. This coalition, empowered by their status, *develops a vision* and a strategy. We suggest this strategy be grounded in implementing one or a few of the high-impact interventions that we described above.

The fourth step of Kotter's process is *communicating the vision*. We know that community colleges tend to have poor communication pathways. We used to be amazed when working with community colleges to learn how little faculty and staff are aware of the institution's strategic plan or vision for the institution. It is not their fault. Leadership has to do a better job of ensuring that the vision, mission, and planning efforts are communicated thoughtfully, thoroughly, and constantly across the institution.

Next, the model focuses on *empowering the people who are to implement the change*, Kotter describes this step as removing obstacles. Empowering educators who are to implement the change will focus them on the process rather than the endgame. Kotter recommends that *short-term wins*—your milestones—can be achieved and must be celebrated to move people forward. For example, reaching consensus on a decision should be celebrated. Building on these short-term wins the vision gains *credibility* and it is easier to move toward the final goal. Finally, Kotter addresses how to *anchor* any new policy or intervention to the existing culture of the institution. Communication is crucial to this work and must be consistent throughout the process.

SUMMARY

In this chapter, we matched many of the student success problems a college faces to the appropriate, associated intervention. We focused on key points in a student's career and research-based, high-impact solutions.

Implementation is not easy work—in many ways, it is art meeting science. Community colleges have lots of issues to address, and knowing which ones to begin with first is a bit more art than science. You turn to science when identifying the policy, program, and instructional supports to implement. But when the work of implementation begins, you need a combination of artful persuasion and scientific strategies grounded in human judgment and decision making and organizational habit.

We concluded by showing that a purposeful and deliberate process, grounded in Kotter's strategies, helps to move student success efforts forward despite resistance. We know that if you embrace a strategy that takes into account your college culture, you can successfully address student success issues.

Monitoring Interventions and Continuous Improvement

It was the end of the three-year grant, and the project team from the college was meeting with the evaluator. Although they had implemented strategies that research had found to be effective, the needle had hardly moved on completion rates at their college. They reviewed the project history and concluded that they had implemented the program faithfully and that the expected number of students had participated. They could not figure out what had gone wrong. Annual reports submitted to the funder in years 1 and 2 showed promise, but this promise was never realized.

■ ■ ■

This is typical of many efforts at community colleges around the country. Programs, policies, and supports are implemented—and implemented well—but they don't produce the anticipated results. We find that many colleges track lagging indicators that describe what is happening but don't give any information about why or how to take action. In this chapter, we present a method for monitoring and adjusting programs using leading indicators that doesn't demand the intense resources of most continuous improvement efforts linked to evaluations.

KEY CONCEPTS FOR ASSESSING INTERVENTIONS

Before we get to the discussion of monitoring and the continuous improvement process, it would be helpful to briefly review some basics. So let's take a quick look at some terms and methods.

What to Monitor: Structure, Process, and Outcome

When monitoring a program, we want to look at three areas. The first, and often overlooked, is the program structure. This includes the relatively stable characteristics of the providers of services, the tools and resources they have at their disposal, and the physical and organizational settings in which they work. The purpose of assessing structure is to ensure that the resources needed to implement the program are available and used efficiently. It also allows for exploration of the ways in which a college environment might not fully support the intervention being implemented. This gets to the issue of fit. Conrad and Roberts-Gray note that "Programs are embedded in and influenced by a surrounding set of conditions and events."[1] This notion of embeddedness can be assessed as the level of fit between your selected interventions and your college culture. For example, in some colleges where we've worked, the lack of fit is evidenced by lack of buy-in—there might have been a few champions who cared deeply about the program or service, but a majority of the faculty and staff had other interests.

The second aspect to monitor is *process*, which we call the set of activities that go on within and between the groups implementing an intervention and the students or target population. Process explores the extent to which an intervention is being delivered as designed. Let's pause for a moment and think about this. We like to frame this issue as a continuum. It is often necessary to adjust an intervention to meet the local context to improve its fit. But at some point, a program could be modified so that it no longer has the key attributes that made it work (see figure 6.1).

FIGURE 6.1   The implementation fidelity dimension

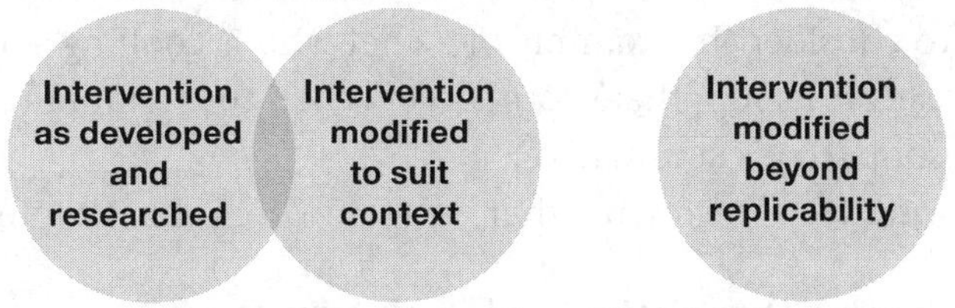

Intervention
as developed
and
researched

Intervention
modified
to suit
context

Intervention
modified
beyond
replicability

Monitoring process also includes reporting on the number of students served and a description of the extent to which implementation meets the project timelines.

The final aspect to monitor is *outcome*—the change in the target population's current and future status that can be attributed to the intervention. Here is where our leading and lagging indicators come into play. These indicators are the expected outcomes—short- and long-term—that are to be measured. Remember, leading indicators are actionable and lead to the lagging indicators (the big goals). For example, if the lagging indicator is persistence for non-majority populations, we know it is important to monitor the leading indicators of course retention and grades. We have found that successful course retention and grades of C or better are correlated with increased persistence.

When We Monitor: Formative and Summative

Often, the teams we work with find the terms formative and summative confusing. They equate formative with process and summative with outcome. In fact, both formative and summative assessments apply to all three areas to be monitored: structure, process, and outcome. Summative assessments occur at a program's end and describe what happened. There is no opportunity to make use of the information to modify or improve interventions. Formative assessments occur during an intervention's life cycle and can be used to shape or redirect it. As Michael Scriven, a noted evaluation theorist and evaluator, described it, "Formative evaluations help to form the program being assessed."[2] Another way to remember the difference between formative and summative is to consider the example of a chef who is cooking soup. When the chef tastes the soup, that's formative. When the restaurant customer tastes the soup, that's summative.

It is formative assessments that we focus on in this chapter.

How We Monitor: Quantitative and Qualitative Data

In monitoring interventions, we collect two types of data: quantitative and qualitative. Quantitative data is the numbers, typically from a college's student information system. These are the metrics used to assess whether or not the intervention is making a difference in the leading and lagging indicators. Quantitative data can do a good job of telling us what happened, but rarely provides insight into how or why. We can see whether or not interventions and policy changes are working; however, numbers alone rarely give us information about what to do. So it is important to collect qualitative data as well.

Qualitative data is descriptive information from project staff, faculty, and students, which often comes from observation, surveys, interviews, focus groups, or artistic depictions. Qualitative data is important because it allows us to get answers to questions that typically plague improvement efforts such as, "Why is our student drop rate so high?" or "Why did so few students take advantage of the freshman year experience?"

CONTINUOUS IMPROVEMENT: A FOUR-STAGE CYCLE

Now that we have the basic concepts in hand, we can turn to the focus of this chapter. Continuous improvement is a gradual, never-ending process that is focused on increasing the effectiveness and/or efficiency of an organization to fulfill its policy and objectives. When educators think of continuous improvement, they can feel overwhelmed because they focus on lagging indicators, which can make it seem like a long and tedious endeavor. The model we present, however, is easy to implement because it is targeted and limited.

We like to use a four-stage continuous improvement cycle—assessment, planning, implementation, and progress monitoring—as the basis for our work (see figure 6.2). Educators we work with find this cycle is easily applied to their interventions and doesn't require a degree or specialization in evaluation research. It doesn't turn a team into skilled evaluators, but it provides all that is required to monitor an intervention and determine if it is working and where to look if it isn't. It begins with assessment, but it doesn't end anywhere. This is the nature of a cycle.

FIGURE 6.2   The four-stage continuous improvement cycle

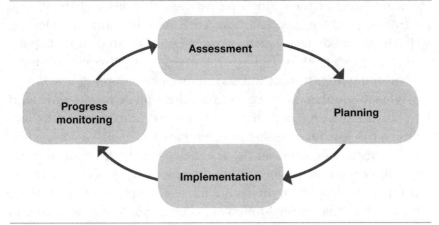

Assessment

Assessment is the determination of the extent of a problem. For example, which groups are underperforming to create a college's achievement gap: first-time-in-college students? In the assessment phase, we ask the following questions:

- What are our key lagging indicators?
- Do the leading indicators we collect relate directly to these lagging indicators?
- Is the information accurate?
- What is the story we need to act on?

These questions address what needs to be measured (leading and lagging indicators), the accuracy of the information being used, and a clear understanding of what the information is saying about the gaps. This stage prepares for implementation by setting the stage for understanding and action.

Typically when we work with a college, we assess four things when deciding which indicators to assess. Our indicators should relate to who the college is serving, student achievement, student engagement, and equity between student groups. That is, we assess capture rates. We look at how students are performing (grades, assessment scores, completion, etc.). Indicators of the connection between students and the college (retention, persistence, satisfaction, etc.) are important to review, as well. Finally, we disaggregate the data to ensure all student subpopulations (e.g., gender, ethnicity, English learners, FTIC, discipline of study) are benefiting from student success improvement efforts.

When beginning the work, the assessment phase provides the tools necessary to move forward. The phase informs planning efforts by providing a baseline for assessing interventions and their outcomes. It is essential to be sure data can be accessed that tells the status of leading indicators for the campus and key subpopulations of interest before starting to implement an intervention. For example, we were working with a college that wanted to look at course enrollment rates early in the semester. They met in September, only to realize that enrollment rates were not finalized until October. When engaging in continuous improvement efforts, be aware of data reporting cycles so the information you need is available when you need it.

After going through the full continuous improvement cycle, a college is back to assessment. In our experience, many colleges adopt a one-and-done approach and do not review their work. But at the turn of a new cycle, it's time to review assessment tools to ensure the right things are being measured—those indicators that inform action. But don't be tempted to drop a program too early. We call this death by pilot. Too often, colleges will not find success in their first implementation effort. Nobody hits a golf ball perfectly the first time they tee it up (if at all). Lagging indicators take time because they're not sensitive enough to show change immediately. And sometimes leading indicators require more than one cycle to show change.

Planning

The second stage of our continuous improvement model is planning. Planning is a method of acting, doing, proceeding, making, etc. that is developed in advance. This means a development and implementation timeline is set before beginning and everyone on the team is aware of their role and the calendar. In the planning phase we ask the following questions:

- Are the actions being considered addressing the problems we're trying to solve?
- Are our planned actions research-based?
- Do we have adequate resources (funding, personnel, facilities)?
- Are we addressing policy, instruction, and support?
- Can we realistically implement these plans?

These questions can be addressed with the information and methods for aligning interventions with problems presented in chapter 5.

There also are two aspects to the planning phase that are crucial and often overlooked: awareness and preparation for implementation monitoring. Let's take a brief look at what we need to plan related to these two sets of activities.

Awareness. Whether educators are aware of the initiative often can make or break an intervention. In our consulting work, we are surprised at how often we come into a college and find that nobody is aware of efforts to address student success issues beyond those faculty, staff, and administrators directly involved. We strongly encourage our community college clients to publicize and market their efforts campuswide. We have found that when they do so, faculty, students, and others who might be interested in participating are more likely to bring their thoughts, ideas, and willingness to work to these efforts. In our experience, publicizing an initiative increases the participation rate because the target student population is aware of the availability of services.

Planning to Monitor Implementation. The planning stage also is a crucial time to decide how the implementation will be monitored.

Developing progress-monitoring plans now will help to ensure a successful process down the road at stage 4. Be sure to schedule points at which various activities will be assessed. Know when surveys will be administered and interviews conducted. This will ensure student and faculty voices are included in reports and provide the necessary feedback for program improvement.

The planning stage also is the time to involve information technology (IT) and institutional research (IR) offices so the data needed to address identified indicators will be available when needed. Sometimes it can be difficult to obtain information related to project indicators. But planning this work helps to ensure there are no surprise requests and reporting needs won't shift down the priority list because a special request comes in from the college president. There are five questions to take to IT/IR:

- What data will be collected?
- When will the data be available and does this match up with reporting and implementation schedules?
- Can data be disaggregated for key subpopulations of interest?
- How will the data be formatted to help us understand what happened?
- Is it possible to compare students who are and are not receiving intervention services?

In our experience, this last item can be most difficult and therefore is most often neglected. It is important to have tracking systems in place. Look at interventions and associated indicators and be sure the implementation and data folks know which data elements from information systems will be used and what metrics can be reported for every one of them.

Unfortunately, campus researchers often are not trained in evaluation (which is different from research), We strongly encourage colleges to hire a qualified evaluator at this point in the cycle. In fact, a common requirement of federal grants is to build in an evaluation budget and hire an external evaluator. After all, since the college has invested considerable time and energy into addressing the problem, it will want to know whether or not its identified intervention successfully did so.

Planning Tools. There are many planning tools available. GANTT charts, for instance, are very useful to illustrate project, task, and subtask start and end dates and can include other information such as who holds primary responsibility for the task, and there are many applications, apps, and other software that facilitate shared project planning and management. Our suggestion is to keep it simple. We like using a template to list tasks, anticipated start date, anticipated end date, actual start date, actual end date, person responsible, and a place for notes. This should be a shared document that all project staff can access using a program, application, or sharing system at your college.

We also encourage planning regular project meetings. Early in the project, plan for frequent meetings that include those responsible for development. We recommend at least two meetings per month (as the project moves along, meetings can be less frequent). Plan for a way, between meetings, for input about project obstacles to be heard, and be ready to hold unanticipated meetings to address these. Make sure there is frequent communication between team members; timely communication helps move projects along.

Implementation

Now we are at the action stage of our continuous improvement model, when interventions are implemented. Implementation means to put into effect according to, or by means of, a defined plan or procedure. It is important to have completed stages 1 and 2 first, so a defined plan or procedure exists for implementation activities.

In our experience, colleges are excellent at planning and poor at implementing. There are two related questions we keep in mind when consulting with colleges during the implementation stage:

- Do the expected implementers have the skills, resources, and supports they need?
- Can the identified practices be implemented faithfully (and how will we know)?

The first question was probably addressed early in project planning. But this is a good time to revisit the issue. Check on the available resources, including human, fiscal, and physical. Human resources include time—if faculty members are involved, can they get released from a teaching assignment to do their work if necessary? Does project development and implementation require travel (e.g., to an initiative meeting organized by the funder)—and what are your college's travel policies? Review the GANTT chart or other project-planning materials and decide if any task dates need to be adjusted due to a late or early project start. Fiscal resources include not only sufficient funding to implement but also to sustain and possibly grow the work. Finally, physical resources include space requirements to support staff and students engaged in the intervention.

The second question is related to stage 4, progress monitoring (discussed below). But, as noted above, it is important to be sure any research-based, highly successful practices are not changed so much that they no longer are being implemented as designed. This also relates to the issue of skills and resources. Lack of knowledge and skills can have a negative impact on faithful implementation.

RASIC. When we work with colleges, we like to use the RASIC tool for implementation. This simple tool helps ensure all action items are addressed by someone; that nothing is slipping through the cracks. You've probably guessed that it's an acronym. The letters stand for:[3]

- **Responsible:** This is the person who owns the task; who has to do the work to achieve the task.
- **Approves:** The person in the *approve* role can be the college president, board, chancellor, department chairs, or any other person who has authority to decide or will be held accountable if the project or the task fails. Typically, this is the person who the responsible person is accountable to. The approver can be there to ensure quality and that the intervention matches the broader institutional culture. He or she also can pave the way for broader approval (e.g., from a board).
- **Supports:** These are the people who assist the responsible individual to get the task done. They may include curriculum developers, boot camp experts, faculty, institutional researchers, and anyone involved in providing resources or doing the development and implementation work.

- **Informed:** These are people who provide input and must be informed of results or actions taken but are not involved in final decision making. A dean is a likely person to fill this role.
- **Consulted:** These are people on campus who provide valuable input into the design of an intervention or assist with implementation— for instance, academic counselors, researchers, or faculty with prior experience. Their buy-in is important for successful implementation.

Figure 6.3 shows a sample RASIC matrix. Major tasks are listed in rows down the left side, and the individuals involved in columns across the top. A RASIC role designator is placed in each cell for individuals involved in the task. Note that some individuals can be involved at multiple RASIC activities for the same task or across different tasks. You can download a nice RASIC template from Excel Made Easy (www.excelmadeeasy.com).

Here are some common rules for creating your RASIC matrix:

- *The Big Rule:* Only one A per task. More will create confusion.
- More than two Rs in the same row means duplication of work.
- No Rs in a row means a there is a gap to be filled or the task is not needed.
- Rs and As in the first columns (left side) of matrix. This improves clarity of the table.

FIGURE 6.3   RASIC matrix example

	Person A	Person B	Person C	Person D	Person E
Task 1.1	R, A	S		I	
Task 1.2	A	R	S	S	C
Task 1.3	A	R	S	I	
Task 2.1	A	R		S	C

Note: R = Responsible; A = Approves; S= Supports; I = Informed; C = Consulted

- One A and one R in every row. The same person can be responsible and accountable.
- If there is a role with no Rs or As, reconsider if the role is needed.

Finally, know your team. You don't want to assign tasks to individuals who won't get the job done. We have worked with colleges that have assigned roles and responsibilities to educators who, for whatever reason, are unable to complete their tasks. It is important to have backups. Identify a secondary R-person for each task who can step up if a team member leaves the project or the college. Without a backup, the project could easily stall.

Progress Monitoring

The fourth stage in our cycle is progress monitoring. Monitoring progress includes judging or determining the significance, worth, or quality of the work. The key word here is judge. It is important to make judgments about interventions, supports, and policies that lead to decisions about whether to maintain them and scale up, modify them, replace them, or abandon them.

We encourage our clients to see abandoning an ineffective practice, after reasonable implementation efforts and monitoring, as a successful outcome. Why continue to waste valuable, scarce resources on an intervention that is not achieving its goals? It can be difficult to drop an intervention that is not effective, especially if it gets high satisfaction ratings. But just because everyone likes something, doesn't mean it is worth keeping.

In the progress monitoring stage, you should ask the following questions:

- Are the original assessment indicators being used?
- Does qualitative data provide us with information about why the intervention is working or not?
- Is the data disaggregated in such a way as to allow us to understand differential impact?
- Can we make a decision to maintain (and scale up), adjust, replace, or eliminate?

Remember, to understand why an intervention is or is not effective, qualitative data from observations, surveys, and interviews is needed. To ensure data is disaggregated to understand differential impact, remember to have negotiated with IR/IT staff during the planning stage to obtain data about key subpopulations.

This is the continuous improvement cycle, so these are going to be formative evaluations that help to form judgments about the program. The purpose is to use leading indicators to assess whether or not student success is being improved as intended and expected. If it is not, go back to the research on high-impact practices for the student success issue being addressed. But, as noted above, don't abandon a project prematurely. Wait for a second assessment cycle (or more) to occur before making any decisions. One cycle might not be representative of the true impact of a program, especially if it's a college's first experience with an intervention. Those delivering the intervention could improve their skills after one year of practice. Also, interventions in the form of policy changes might take a while to demonstrate their effects.

How and Where to Correct. If progress monitoring reveals that indicator targets are not being met, it is important to look for reasons why. As we've noted before, check the fidelity of implementation. We have found this to be the number-one reason for poor outcomes. This investigation needs to be approached as a team effort and not a witch-hunt, which we find leads to implementers claiming fidelity that isn't there. Coming from a position of trying to discover why by looking at indicators rather than individuals assumes a willingness to make change to improve the program and that people will not be punished for less-than-stellar outcomes. This supports conversations about fidelity and the continuum of modification.

Another thing to check when interventions do not go as planned is which students are participating in the interventions and if the target populations are being reached. Be sure to interview students eligible for an intervention who did not participate. A lot can be learned from them—possibly more than from participants—about target populations' views of the intervention and its likely impact, the success of marketing to students, why students dropped out of the intervention, and more.

Review your college's policies; and not just the ones that might have changed. In our experience, sometimes policies stand in the way of an intervention's success. For example, students might not be able to register for the interventions they need at the time they need them due to competing priority registration rules.

SUMMARY

Engaging in a continuous improvement cycle is a way of managing the development and implementation of an intervention that increases its likelihood of success. It should not add work to the process; if done right, the cycle should reduce duplication of effort and resource consumption.

We recommend a four-stage cycle that moves from assessment to planning to implementation to progress monitoring, and then begins again with an assessment. There are specific questions to be addressed and methods for moving through each stage. Some methods are grounded in templates and standard practices (e.g., GANTT charts, RASIC matrixes) and other methods are simply best practices.

By adopting this cycle, a college can confirm its interventions are working efficiently and, most likely, effectively toward addressing student success issues.

PART 3

Case Studies of Data-Use Reforms

Engaging Stakeholders with Data

Long Beach City College

Lauren Davis Sosenko

Long Beach City College (LBCC) has long been an evidence-driven institution. Its Office of Institutional Effectiveness (IE) continually looks for ways to adopt lessons from the larger field to unearth insights locally that result in student success. One such data-driven student intervention is multiple measures placement using high school transcript data. LBCC adopted this practice in fall 2012 and has offered higher-level placements to thousands of students who would have otherwise been placed at lower levels with traditional methods. In addition to using data for direct student interventions, IE—in collaboration with faculty, staff, and administrators—seeks evidence on an ongoing basis to support decision making and improvement within the college. This chapter will highlight the recent data-use techniques applied at LBCC through its new strategic plan. It will provide context about LBCC, describe why data use is integral to the strategic plan, and then explain how LBCC stakeholders are refining its measures, setting targets, and making connections to individuals' work. The chapter will close with a description of preliminary observations and next steps in this ongoing process.

LONG BEACH CITY COLLEGE COMMUNITY AND CONTEXT

Long Beach City College, located in the coastal urban city of Long Beach in Southern California, serves about twenty-five thousand students each term. The college was established in 1927, and has two campuses—the Liberal Arts Campus (LAC) located in the north-central part of Long Beach, and the Pacific Coast Campus, located on the western side of the city. The district serves 129 square miles of diverse localities in the Long Beach area, including neighborhoods in Lakewood, Signal Hill, and Avalon.[1] The Long Beach economy has been thriving over the last several years. Despite large aviation production leaving the region, the Port of Long Beach buoys the local economy, providing thousands of high-paying jobs in the city. Other important industry markets are manufacturing, health care, and retail trade.[2]

Over the last three years, LBCC has been a majority Hispanic–serving institution. Fifty-eight percent (58 percent) of LBCC students identify as Hispanic/Latino, 14 percent as white, 12 percent as African American, 12 percent as Asian, and 4 percent as other ethnicities.[3] Many LBCC students are first-generation college students (the college conservatively estimates that about 60 percent of LBCC students are first-generation college-going). Further, half of all LBCC students demonstrate significant financial need (50 percent of incoming students qualify for the Board of Governor's fee waiver based on demonstrated financial need).[4] The college is constantly considering how to better support students, because many LBCC students face serious personal hardships; for example, in fall 2015, LBCC estimated that one in six students struggle with housing instability while pursuing their studies.[5]

LBCC offers degrees and certificates in over sixty areas of study taught by 682 full-time and 682 part-time faculty.[6] Most recently, LBCC faculty have been adopting associate degrees for transfer (ADTs) in twenty disciplines.[7] These degrees are aligned with the California State University degree requirements and streamline the transfer experience for students who intend to move on to a public four-year university. Degree attainment continues to grow at LBCC, and most of the growth is attributed to ADTs. In 2015–2016, LBCC awarded 1,213 degrees, a 9 percent increase from the year before. The student demand for degrees aligned to four-year bachelor's degree expectations is clear.

Like many community colleges across the country, most LBCC students place into basic skills in math, reading, and English. Once students are in basic skills, few progress out of these courses into college- or transfer-level courses in those subjects. Faculty at the college are working on several important methods to accelerate instruction in basic skills or use technology to more effectively teach these courses, but have yet to scale these innovations to the population of basic skills students.[8] For example, LBCC uses acceleration and technological products to modularize the curriculum and provide timely student deficit information to faculty.

LBCC has partnered with its feeder high school district Long Beach Unified School District and the California State University, Long Beach, for many years, and formalized this alliance in 2008 as the Long Beach College Promise. The program started as an agreement between the educational CEOs in the city to support local student success across the educational pipeline. Through the Promise, our institutions collaboratively consider policies that will support local student success and coordinate projects to support student transitions from one school to another. In 2014, the City of Long Beach joined the Promise as a trusted partner focused on industry connections and creating internship opportunities for Long Beach youth.[9] Most recently, the Promise partners are developing defined pathways for students from high school through university in liberal arts, business administration, health, education, life and physical sciences, and engineering, with funding from the Governor's Innovation Award.[10]

While the growth of degree awards and strong partner collaboration continues, the last several years have also been a time of renewal for the college after the deep cuts made during the financial downturn in 2010–2011. Throughout the last two years, LBCC has hired new full-time and part-time faculty. The fresh faculty voice and work by many stakeholders around the college to revitalize the climate have had a marked shift in the college culture. Most notable of these is faculty engagement in developing the college's strategic plan. Further, critical investments in equity and student supports spotlight and fund opportunities to better serve our most vulnerable students.

EVERYONE'S NEW STRATEGIC PLAN

In fall 2016, LBCC started to implement its new strategic plan, which many stakeholders had a part in crafting, and now implementing. The Strategic Plan Oversight Taskforce (SPOT) named the plan "Be the Change"—meaning that plan for everyone at the college would be part of the change needed for our students.[11] Relying heavily on the Community College Research Center's (CCRC) Redesigning America's Community Colleges, LBCC set out to dramatically improve its completion rate by guiding students more quickly into a field of study and supporting them to achieve their educational goals.[12] The Office of Institutional Effectiveness had already been using aspects of the IEBC data-use model with stakeholders across the campus, but the strategic plan launch has provided an important opportunity to engage many more stakeholders in quality data use.

The plan has four major goals:

1. Accelerate and close gaps in the equitable achievement of students' educational and career goals.
2. Improve and accelerate college readiness for all student groups.
3. Cultivate a climate of respect, inclusion, and support for our internal and external communities and lead efforts to innovate and align resources that impact the educational, economic, and social outcomes for our Long Beach communities.
4. Focus institutional resources on the structures, processes, and practices that support transformation.[13]

The strategic plan includes twenty-one metrics. These are organized around the student phases of progression through the community college highlighted in the Completion by Design initiative's *Understanding the Student Experience Framework* to measure how well the college is meeting its overarching goals.[14] The LBCC strategic plan metrics start with leading indicators that the college identified as antecedents to the lagging measures of completion and/or transition:

- **Connection:** Measures how well students are applying and enrolling in the college.
- **Entry:** Measures how students are completing key gatekeeper courses, such as transfer-level math and English, and how many students are demonstrating an intention to complete an award at LBCC.
- **Progress:** Assesses how well and quickly students are moving toward a completion.

Finally, the strategic plan metrics include two lagging indicators:

- **Completion:** The traditional lagging indicator of college success, which measures how many students are reaching the finish line by earning a degree or certificate and how quickly they are doing so.
- **Transition:** This final domain measures how well students are moving on to a university or workplace.

With the metrics set in a way that college leaders can identify key areas for action using the leading measures under Connection, Entry, and Progress, the SPOT team expressed a need to ensure that the strategic plan is the blueprint for all stakeholders at the college. They have worked tirelessly to ensure that everyone who wanted a voice in the direction of the college had the opportunity to weigh in about the development of the plan, as well as how to realize the plan during the first implementation phase. Another strategy SPOT is using to engage stakeholders in the plan is through data use, and IE has taken the lead to integrate data use into initial first steps of target development and into data produced to support existing processes like department planning and program review.

Integrating leading and lagging indicators into department planning and program review is just one of the current efforts to build strong data-use strategies at LBCC. LBCC has been building capacity to strengthen its analytic offerings to increase the visibility of data to more stakeholders—ensuring that the right people have the right data to make timely decisions about their work. IE has changed its data reporting processes to provide more easily digestible data reports than have been provided in the past. IE staff design these reports to highlight findings and support interpretation for the college community. They use data practices such as labeling charts with findings or focusing data presentations on key audiences' perspectives from the IEBC data-use model. IE staff are also applying other data-use techniques such as strategically using color and limiting distracting content in charts from Cole Nussbaumer Knaflic's *Storytelling with Data*.[15]

In addition to creating concise and directed reports, IE is working on drill-down dashboards using Tableau technology that will cater to multiple stakeholder audiences and offer key enhancements to the department planning and program review data packets that faculty can vet for content and usability. Further, LBCC invested in Civitas business intelligence software to expand its use of predictive analytics. In the coming year, LBCC's Civitas work group will explore this platform to understand what key predictive insights may inform the strategic plan's implementation and highlight new leading indicators for the college to monitor moving forward.

Strategic Plan Metric Development and Establishing Targets

LBCC is continuing to use the IEBC data-use model components of analytics, human judgment and decision making, and organizational habits. LBCC is using these data use concepts in three ways to engage and empower stakeholders and connect them to the strategic plan. First, the original metric definitions in the high-level dashboard focus on leading and lagging indicators, ensuring that actionable data is identified for leadership. Second, faculty and staff are engaged in reviewing the baseline data of the metrics and setting targets. SPOT identified stakeholders based on their role at the college and perspective to participate in the target-setting conversation. For example, outreach staff and communications are helping to describe the context of Connection, while our transfer counselor will be among those discussing the Transition metrics. Finally, IE will provide faculty and staff with guidance to align program, department, and service unit success measures to the strategic plan metrics focusing on appropriate leading and lagging metrics for each department. This integration of data use into existing processes for continuous improvement will support strong organizational habits around data use.

Strategic Plan Metric Definitions

In spring 2016, LBCC sent a team to a preconference session of the American Association of Community Colleges about guided pathways. During this event, Rob Johnstone and Davis Jenkins gave a talk on the "The State of Guided Pathways Reform Efforts," telling the story of Georgia State University's efforts to understand why its students were not completing.[16] Georgia State had traditionally used persistence and completion metrics; the former showed very high fall-to-fall enrollment, but the university did not see this high persistence translate into completions. In response to these observations, the university decided to not just measure persistence, but to also integrate a "sophomore standing" leading indicator to better understand how students were progressing in their first year. It found that the vast majority of their students, despite re-enrolling in the subsequent fall, were not making the expected progress toward sophomore status.[17] The university was able to focus efforts on the students' first-year experience to increase student progress; this ultimately improved student completion, and also eliminated the achievement gap between different ethnicity groups.[18]

When the LBCC team shared this story back at home, it was an "Aha!" moment for staff working on the new strategic plan, which was heavily inspired by the guided pathways work. Community colleges do not traditionally measure students' progress in a way that considers if students are taking the *right* units, only that they are taking units. The California Community College Scorecard includes a thirty-unit measure, but those can be any thirty units. Many LBCC students are completing tens of units in basic skills courses; therefore this metric really tells only a partial story about how well students are progressing. The SPOT team decided to integrate new metrics into the strategic plan to measure how well students are completing their degree-applicable units within specific time frames.

Defining these new metrics can be tricky, because a halfway point is not consistently defined at the community college level. Nevertheless, using the LBCC "Intent to Complete" cohort (a standard threshold defined by the California Community College Chancellor's Office that includes any student who earns six units and attempts math or English; these students' course-taking behavior signals that they are attending college to earn a degree, certificate, or transfer), the college is now tracking its own form of "sophomore standing." This metric is defined as how many students earn thirty transferrable units with nine units within a specific subject area within eighteen months. IE determined, based on analysis of past completers, that most students who end up with a completion hit this critical threshold by their midpoint, rather than a lower number of concentrated units by students who have not yet determined their goal. This rate of progress would put a student on track for completion in a three-year time period.

The college also has adopted a more assertive expectation for our students to finish more quickly. Strategic plan metrics include the percentage of students who earn forty units, with twelve units in a specific subject area, within two- and four-year time periods. These measures are an aggressive departure from measuring students in a six-year time frame.

In addition to the new set of Progress metrics, LBCC has also defined metrics for Connection and Entry. The Connection metrics also are a new lens for the college, including the percentage of students who enroll out of all who apply, the percentage of seniors in our service area who enroll at LBCC, and the percentage of incoming students who are deemed "college ready." Entry metrics include measures of basic skills participation and success that the college has tracked for many years. However, LBCC also is reviewing how many students are obtaining student educational plans and when they are getting these plans. LBCC believes all of these indicators will have an impact on our college completion and transition measures.

TARGET SETTING

In the first year of the strategic plan's rollout, stakeholders who are deeply involved within a domain of student experience (e.g., connection, entry, progress, completion, or transition) are reviewing LBCC's last five years of data on each metric, providing their perspective about what these data mean, interpreting where untenable gaps are in the narrative of the student experience (i.e., determining where to add or revise a metric), and finally, considering ways to align their own service unit outcomes with leading metrics that will have an impact on the strategic plan metrics. During these reviews, participants have been learning about the metrics, the leading and lagging framework, and the college's intention to build alignment into its review processes so that all stakeholders can see their place in the plan and can align their success measures to how the college is measuring its success.

To date, these engaging conversations have focused on four key themes. First, participants are reviewing definitions to ensure they understand what the data is saying. This is of particular importance in the Progress domain, because the college is using new metrics that are unfamiliar to LBCC stakeholders. For example, during one review session, IE described "sophomore status" and a participant asked, "Why do we not consider when students are sophomores?" and other participants wondered, "Is a nine-unit concentration demonstrating student focus when some courses may be four or five units?" The college will consider these types of questions when refining metrics.

Second, participants are discussing what the baseline data are saying about how students are experiencing LBCC. The data elicit many more questions about how students are using our current processes and how the college is designed to support student connection, entry, and progress. Third, participants are trying to decipher "what it will take" to change the student experience to a degree that students' behavior will result in movement on the metrics. At this point, they consider how they will be empowered by college leadership to work differently in their roles to realize the strategic plan's goals. Finally, participants are considering targets and the rationale behind them, as well as other considerations to meet these targets for the larger SPOT team to consider.

In an effort to focus data use, the target-setting meetings are limited to only metrics within one student experience domain and are limited to participants who have a perspective on that student experience. However, participants discuss relationships between different domains and data points that inform target setting. For example, if the group is considering progress toward completion the group must consider changes to basic skills course sequence completion (e.g., throughput) as well as some enrollment management data points, such as how many course sections have been offered over time. Through this process, participants are exploring the relationships with the leading and lagging indicators in question.

This process is taking longer to identify targets than anyone anticipated. However, the conversations between participants about how they personally can contribute to "Being the Change" is exactly the movement that the SPOT team hoped to establish through this planning process. For example, one participant described a marketing campaign that his department could initiate to target all students who apply to the college, but do not enroll. Further, participants are identifying how early changes in student connection may influence later services related to the student experience. For instance, participants wondered, if the number of students enrolling increased, how would the college ensure that all new students receive student education plans or have the capacity to provide basic skills education when appropriate? SPOT is summarizing these deep conversations to flesh-out the strategic plan implementation phase that will impact the entire institution and to inform leadership about what critical supports LBCC faculty and staff need to realize this work.

CONSIDERING PERSPECTIVE AND USING EXISTING IMPROVEMENT PROCESSES

LBCC is purposefully targeting human judgment and decision making, as well as organizational habit to integrate its strategic plan into existing processes for multiple types of stakeholders. Different levels of data are important to inform different types of student success questions. When considering collegewide policy change or the culmination of all strategic efforts, the "big picture" level of data is essential to consider. These views are already available on the LBCC Student Success Scorecard and will be integrated into a strategic plan dashboard.

Many important decisions are happening within LBCC departments and classrooms that directly impact student success. To support these decisions, IE intends to work with each department as they develop discipline- and course-specific leading and lagging indicators to include in both department planning and program review. These indicators will be aligned with the LBCC Strategic Plan Dashboard metrics, but they would be specific to department/faculty contexts and perspectives.

The strategic plan calls for action at all levels of the college, including department reflection and action to improve outcomes. If we want to empower individual departments and faculty to contribute to the strategic plan we must provide data that is relevant to the work those stakeholders contribute (figure 7.1). Therefore, integration of leading and lagging indicators from the continuum are important for faculty to consider in their planning.

FIGURE 7.1   Leading and lagging indicator examples by different levels of data

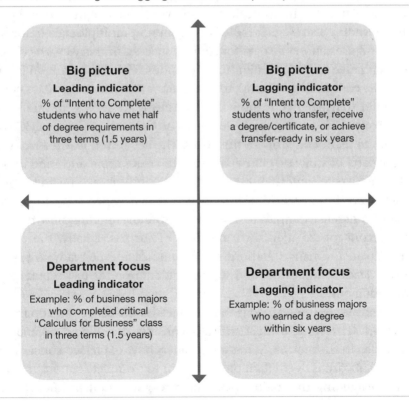

WHERE ARE WE NOW?

The strategic plan implementation and the corresponding data use work is still in its early stage. IE staff are currently convening faculty/staff groups to consider the plan metrics and to frame the leading and lagging concept of the dashboard metrics themselves. During these meetings IE staff are working with staff to identify targets for the metrics and infusing the idea to create alignment with program, department, and service unit outcomes. However, the opportunity to fully engage in the planning cycle will take time as more faculty and staff learn about the new tools and support that IE will provide. This work will begin in earnest in the 2017–2018 and 2018–2019 academic years.

LBCC intends to see alignment of college measures in all plans. As many stakeholders work to define their own measures of success, IE will support each group to see how to best align individual departments with the big picture of the strategic plan. IE will also facilitate conversations about leading and lagging indicators to support multiple stakeholders to find and use actionable data for student success. In this way, the college will enhance its commitment to continuous improvement at all levels.

The college also will work to increase the visibility of key data points to build transparency in how it is measuring its success to build trust and consistency among stakeholders. Through this process, LBCC continues to learn and grow in this work. The key lesson learned from the early parts of strategic plan data use is to create room and time for key stakeholders to understand the purpose behind the leading and lagging framework for data use. IE has learned that it is necessary to provide many concrete examples to assist users in understanding how to apply these concepts to their own measures of success. Finally, the college must plan for many iterations of key metrics and be ready to explore many leading indicators and supporting data points to support target development.

Another lesson learned is that the metrics the college sets do impact its work. Therefore, it must critically consider the student populations included in the metrics. Some stakeholders have expressed concern that the dashboard is overreliant on the Intent to Complete cohort, in many cases excluding the majority of students who enroll in LBCC classes who are not seeking completion, but who are gaining benefit from the institution. LBCC's SPOT is considering ways to expand this view while still honoring the plan's vision to increase completions.

LBCC and IE strive to learn from these lessons and provide high-quality support for their community of users in linking success measures to the student experience across the college. IE looks forward to integrating these practices into sustainable continuous improvement processes across its campuses and raising the visibility of this data use with key tools like Tableau and Civitas.

EIGHT

Data in the Service of Equity

Southwestern College

Angelica Suarez

In this chapter Angelica Suarez, Vice President of Student Services at Southwestern College, describes how their student equity planning committee made use of our data use model to develop and implement interventions dedicated to improving student equity and success.

LEGISLATIVE CONTEXT

In January 2011, the California Community Colleges Chancellor's Office (CCCCO) convened the Student Success Task Force (SSTF), composed of key stakeholders in the California community colleges, to identify best practices in community colleges focused on student success and completion. The SSTF developed twenty-two recommendations within multiple focus areas targeted at: increasing college and career readiness, strengthening support for entering students, aligning course offerings to meet student needs, improving education of basic skills students, revitalizing and reenvisioning professional development, increasing the coordination among colleges, and aligning resources with student success recommendations. In 2012, Senate Bill 1456 (Seymour-Campbell Student Success Act of 2012) put many of the SSTF recommendations into legislation, and several recommendations were implemented through regulatory changes issued by the California Community College Board of Governors. In essence, the Student Success Act of 2012 provided the foundation to implement several of the SSTF recommendations. More specifically, it set goals to increase the number of community college students who earn a degree or certificate, or transfer to a four-year institution; restructure delivery of student support services to intentionally engage students at the beginning of their educational experience; and direct funding to core services such as orientation, assessment, and counseling and advising to assist students with targeted educational planning. These efforts, designed to not only increase student access to higher education but also increase student success and completion, became known as the Student Success Initiative.

Embedded in this initiative (and the Student Success Act) was the development of a student equity plan by fall 2014 that required community colleges to analyze data to identify achievement gaps and develop targeted interventions to close student achievement in underrepresented groups, thus ensuring access, success, and equity for all students (Education Code 78216 (c)(7)). Data on student outcomes must be disaggregated in eight areas:

- Service area
- Age
- Ethnicity
- Gender

- SES
- Disability
- Foster youth
- Veteran status

The CCCCO describes the student equity planning efforts metrics as follows:

> The student equity plan focuses on increasing access, course completion, ESL and basic skills completion, degrees, certificates and transfer for all students as measured by success indicators linked to the CCC Student Success Scorecard and other measures developed

in consultation with local colleges. "Success indicators" are used to identify and measure areas for which disadvantaged populations may be impacted by issues of equal opportunity. Each college develops specific goals/outcomes and actions to address disparities that are discovered, disaggregating data for indicators by student demographics, preferably in program review. College plans must describe the implementation of each indicator, as well as policies, activities and procedures as they relate to student equity at the college. Student equity plans are prepared with three- to five-year timeframes in terms of planned activities and improvements, to align with the Student Success and Support Program Plan, but must be updated annually.[1]

Further, the CCCCO notes that "While the CCC Board of Governors . . . has made student equity planning a minimum standard for receipt of state funding since 1996 and has long recognized the importance of student equity, until the passage of the Student Success Act of 2012, student equity was not tied to any categorical program and did not receive formal funding through the legislative budget process." In January 2014, the governor's 2014–2015 budget appropriated $70 million to colleges. This funding was increased in the 2015–2016 budget to $137 million and continued with the same level of funding for the 2016–2017 fiscal year.

SOUTHWESTERN COLLEGE CONTEXT

Southwestern Community College District (SCCD) is a two-year educational institution comprising one college and three comprehensive educational centers, commonly referred to as Southwestern College (SWC). The current population of the SCCD service area is estimated to be 499,917, with the SCCD serving approximately twenty thousand students every term. The college is the only institution of higher education located in the southern portion of San Diego County. Its unique location, on a 156-acre plot between the City of San Diego and the US-Mexico international border, positions it to play an important role in the intellectual growth of this region, with 60 percent of the service area population being Hispanic, 12 percent Asian, and 4 percent African American. The college's student population mirrors the communities served by the college. As a Hispanic-serving institution (HSI), the college's largest single ethnic minority are Hispanic (49 percent), with 28 percent white, 9.74 percent Filipino, 5.93 percent African American, 2.47 percent Asian, 1.72 percent American Indian/Alaskan Native, and 1.16 percent Pacific Islander.[2]

As the college enthusiastically engaged in student equity planning efforts in late spring 2014, we recognized the importance of utilizing an integrated planning approach to build on the college's student success agenda begun in spring 2013. That year, the college developed a student success and completion agenda that identified three core interventions to increase student success and completion. These centered on leveraging technology to provide students with responsive education planning tools, an in-depth review of degree and certificate completion to identify and remove barriers to success, and the creation of a first-year experience program. On this foundation—and to facilitate college-wide collaboration, develop synergy between the college's student success initiatives, and leverage resources—the student equity planning committee included representatives from the various constituency groups and areas engaged in student success initiatives similar to the Student Success and Support Program (SSSP), Basic Skills Initiative (BSI), and later, our new HSI Title V Grant, which were already in place. It was important for the college to develop a student equity plan that demonstrated a direct connection between the various institutional initiatives, aligned with the college's strategic priorities, and cohesively and collaboratively increased student success by braiding in the student success initiatives listed above. This approach allowed us to focus on the needs of the student throughout the educational journey, where the various initiatives provided support, and where additional opportunities for support existed along that journey.

An inclusive student equity committee was established in spring 2014, chaired by a faculty member identified by the Academic Senate, the Vice President for Academic Affairs, and the Vice President for Student Affairs. A challenge we faced was to ensure that we identified interventions that focused on systemic institutional changes designed to have the greatest impact in moving the needle of student success. We knew that this would be a difficult task, given that we were dealing with over seven years of cuts to programs and services necessitated by the reduction in state funding. California was in recession, as was much of the country, since 2008. The loss of revenue meant that many faculty and administrative staff had to reduce or eliminate programs and services that they had started and overseen. There was significant interest in restoring these programs now that funding was available.

To address the funding issue and focus on moving the needle, the committee needed to focus exclusively on institutional interventions that would be most effective, delivered at scale. Complicating this work was the fact that funding for student equity had not yet been identified by the state. Planning committees often focus on the available funding and determining what can be done with available resources. We took a different approach: focusing the development of what would serve students best, rather than funding, thus using planning to drive financial decisions.

DEVELOPING THE EQUITY PLAN

Bringing in a Facilitator

The committee had several meetings to discuss the requirements of the student equity plan, the requirements from the CCCCO, and the various data sources available at the college and Statewide. The task of reviewing the considerable amount of data for the various student success indicators (e.g., access, course completion, ESL and basic skills completion, degree and certificate completion, and transfer) in a meaningful way was challenging. Therefore, pinpointing the most critical data elements and achievement gaps became a stumbling block to identifying interventions that would have the most impact on student success.

Recognizing the importance of maintaining an institutional lens in the development of a student equity plan that would focus on interventions inside and outside of the classroom, the college considered the need for an outside facilitator to guide the committee in this critical work. Given IEBC's long history of working with colleges in California and other states in equity planning and engaging faculty, staff, and students in meaningful, data-informed dialogue about student success, we engaged IEBC to facilitate the development of the plan.

The Setup

The committee membership was strategically identified to include faculty from the key areas addressed in the student equity plan—math; English; ESL; counseling; library; tutoring; Disabled Student Services (DSS); extended opportunities, programs and services (EOPS); admissions; finance; research; institutional technology; and staff development. The committee began meeting regularly in the summer of 2014 with the IEBC facilitator. In these meetings, members engaged in meaningful and thoughtful dialogue focused on identifying achievement gaps by reviewing the data, reviewing current practices/interventions at the college, and identifying high-impact, research-based interventions designed to increase student success and equity for the targeted populations outlined in the plan.

Establishing the Role and Approach

Before engaging in the work of developing the student equity plan, the facilitator worked with the committee to develop a common understanding and agreement on the work to be accomplished, and the role of the committee.

The committee agreed that its role was to:

- Review data and determine gaps in student performance
- Engage in discussions around developing the institutional response
- Develop the student equity plan for the CCCCO
- Advocate for the activities to the greater college community

And most important in setting the stage for a student-centered dialogue, the facilitator suggested using a priming technique. Every meeting began with committee members sharing briefly—thirty seconds or less—what they had done during the week to improve student success at Southwestern College. These shared positive stories had the result of strengthening the work of the committee by reinforcing members' important role on the committee and keeping the focus on student success.

The IEBC approach lent itself to committee members feeling invested in the goals of the committee, which ultimately were focused on developing meaningful interventions to close student achievement gaps. The committee used a multiphase approach to identify the goals and activities (interventions) designed to affect systemic change that ultimately led to student success. Over the course of several meetings, the committee members focused on addressing the following components:

- Understanding of student equity requirements (Chancellor's Office template) and the planning process
- Introduction of the data on the five student success factors and identified student achievement gaps
- Participation in an interactive activity (World Café) that allowed the members to:
  - Review and engage with the data (what is the data telling us (achievement gaps); and what else do we need to know)
  - Identify current institutional barriers to student success
  - Identify current institutional practices/interventions that contribute to student success (research-based interventions)
- Establishment of criteria for identifying high-impact interventions
- Identification of high-impact interventions to address achievement gaps
- Development of an implementation plan

Given that one of the challenges faced by the committee in the early stages was making sense of the different data points, the facilitator reformatted the data in ways to aid in the committee's understanding and interpretation (figure 8.1).

This new format added great clarity to understanding the issues. For example, the title of the left slide in 8.1—informing the group that the Hispanic population is underserved by the college—led us to want to study why that is occurring. In fact, the college commissioned an image study to ascertain the disparity.

In the second set of slides (the example shown in the right slide in figure 8.1), the group began to talk about the challenges students faced in completing basic skills curriculum. The committee later went on to recommend supplemental instruction in every basic skills class.

FIGURE 8.1   Reformatting data for clarity

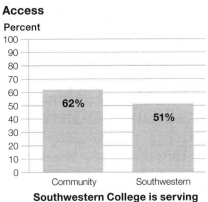

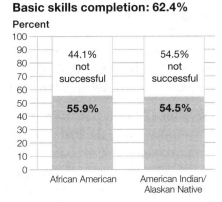

In an effort to engage with the data and share diverse observations, committee members used a fun activity, a World Café event, to help the committee connect, engage, and gain meaning from the data. During the activity, tables were set up according to the student success factors (access, course completion, etc.) with the most important data presented in a user-friendly format.

Committee members rotated to a different table every ten minutes to allow everyone to weigh in on each area. At each table, committee members worked in groups to "engage with the data" and answer a series of questions that included the following:

- What does the data show?
- Where are the specific gaps?
- What more do we need to know?
- What is SWC currently doing to address the areas needing improvement?

At the end of this activity, each table reported out, and several themes began to emerge, as well as potential interventions.

As we began to consider potential interventions, the facilitator discussed the importance of considering leading and lagging indicators when deciding on which to use. This was of particular importance when discussing which interventions would have the greatest impact on the achievement gap. In a review of the data, the committee determined that many of the student success indicators—e.g., degree and certificate completion, transfer—were lagging indicators, and if we wanted to have a significant impact on the student success rates in these areas, we would need to focus on the leading indicators, which included access and basic skills completion, course retention, and course success.

In terms of access, students transitioning from the local high school district were placing in basic skill classes (80 percent for basic skills math; and 37 percent for basic skills English); and once they enrolled in basic skills, their completion rate was 62 percent. Essentially, if students were not able to successfully complete and transition from the basic skills program to the college-level program, then the likelihood that they would complete a degree, certificate, or transfer (lagging indicators) was less likely to occur.

As part of the process of identifying high-impact, focused, and scalable interventions based on research and institutional practice, the committee had numerous discussions about the type of interventions that would be most successful, which is where we experienced the most diversity of thought. While the college has implemented many successful interventions serving thirty to fifty students at the time, we discussed the magnitude of our task in addressing the achievement gaps (in particular, with basic skills). Given that the college has a significant number of students placing in basic skills and a 62 percent success rate, the focus needed to be on interventions that would support the greatest number of students, thus having the greatest potential for closing achievement gaps.

Once the data was reviewed, the committee determined what challenges they wanted to focus on. As a result of much dialogue, the committee reached consensus on the criteria for identifying the interventions that would make the most significant impact on student success across all factors:

- No small, nonscalable interventions
- No small grants for innovation
- Think big, start small
- Not about restoring what was lost in the cuts
- Must be able to go to scale
- Must be research-based
- Must be able to be implemented properly
- Must be adequately resourced
- Think systemically
- Moderate gains can be made with student services alone; big gains can be made with instructional interventions combined with student services
- Leverage resources and impact of other funding sources and initiatives

Once the criteria were established, the committee methodically discussed interventions by focusing on current interventions that met the criteria (in particular, the ability to scale), and national best practices in community colleges for closing student achievement gaps. The committee examined resources from the Community College Research Center and the Center for Community College Student Engagement. Additionally, dialogue at the governing board's Student Success Summit in fall 2014 further informed the committee's discussion of best practices.

Through this thoughtful and meaningful dialogue with the committee in the summer and fall of 2014, the committee identified goals, interventions, and outcomes using a multiphased approach that began with a thorough review of the data to identify specific gaps in student performance across various success indicators (access, course completion, ESL, basic skills completion, degree and certificate completion, and transfer). The process resulted in an understanding that although significant achievement gaps existed in certain student success outcomes when disaggregated by ethnicity, age, gender, socioeconomic status, and disability, overall low completion rates existed across all student success factors.

The committee focused on identifying interventions designed to improve the success of the particular student populations with low completion rates, but ultimately to focus on the overall improvement of student success rates across all factors of success. Consequently, interventions were conceived of at scale, embedding tutoring in specific courses that enroll the majority of the target populations (basic skills and gatekeeper courses), providing faculty and staff with professional development opportunities (focused on basic skills success strategies, cultural competence, and creating inclusive and diverse environments), strengthening support for learning communities and foster youth, creating an institutional culture focused on university transfer (for those students interested in transfer), and enhancing access to the college for underrepresented groups through the improvement of the college's image in the community (SWC as a first-choice educational institution) and intentional formal partnerships with the feeder high school district.

These interventions were in essence "big bets" geared toward effecting systemic institutional change aimed at closing the student achievement gaps for the target populations and raising the achievement and completion rates. They were designed to be focused, intentional, scalable, and high-impact, as well as to effect change across student success factors, rather than each factor individually.

To provide the necessary sustainable infrastructure that allows for the integration of all institutional efforts focused on creating equity-minded, inclusive, and diverse environments designed to advance student success by closing achievement gaps, the college established the Office of Equity, Diversity and Inclusion (EDI).

FAST FORWARD

As the student equity plan enters its final year of implementation (three-year plan) and SWC prepares to develop a new plan, the college is engaged in the evaluation process for the current interventions. A significant portion of the funding has been targeted toward interventions that close achievement gaps for students in basic skills. These interventions include, as mentioned above, partnering with our local high school district, embedding tutors in basic skills courses, and providing faculty, staff, and administrators with professional development opportunities to support the development of a culturally aware, inclusive, and equitable environment for students to succeed.

One of the most essential interventions to bolster student access to higher education included the strengthening of the partnership with our local high school district. This critical partnership was mutually developed to increase college readiness for students. In spring 2016, the college and school district jointly established the South County Education Collaborative focused on the alignment of high school exit expectations with college entrance expectations for English and math. This collaborative was designed to improve student preparedness to succeed in college, increase college-going rates, and improve college completion rates crucial to improving student success in South San Diego County. In fall 2016, faculty teams from both educational systems presented their findings as a result of this gap analysis with corresponding action plans designed to align curriculum in math and English.

An additional large-scale intervention included the implementation of a very successful embedded tutoring program that is currently the largest in the state. A program that began with approximately twelve to eighteen sections of embedded tutoring in basic skills courses, is now offered in over one hundred basic skills and gatekeeper courses. Courses with embedded tutors have resulted in higher levels of student success.

SUMMARY

Our work in fall 2014, focused on developing a state-mandated report, resulted in a transformational shift in how we, as a college committee and college leaders, approached other planning initiatives. Understanding our role as committee members, advocating for our work, and supporting each other in our collective recommendations (even when our own individual idea was not selected) was at the core of building a supportive climate. The approach used by the IEBC facilitator is one that continues to be alive in the work of this committee. Current and former committee members can be heard during different college meetings asking questions of scalability, program fidelity, and data-informed research to support new programs or interventions. Developing institutional synergy across all student success plans by leveraging resources was in large part a result of the work that began with the student equity planning process. The college continues to build on that valuable work to provide equitable educational experiences intentionally designed to close achievement gaps and promote a greater level of student success and completion.

NINE

Leading and Lagging Indicators in Action

Odessa College

Gregory Williams and Don Wood

Odessa College is a Hispanic-serving institution. Over 75 percent of the student body attends college part-time and 35 percent qualify for Pell grants. For more than six decades since the college's founding in 1946, Odessa College's student success was unremarkable, with single-digit graduation rates and double-digit dropout rates. Over the past five years, however, a remarkable change has taken place in the college-going, college-completion behavior of this predominantly minority, socioeconomically disadvantaged, working-class student body.

Without exception, every single disaggregated student group at Odessa College has achieved record levels of success. Historic gaps in class completion, course success, and graduation between underrepresented and underserved students and other groups are closing or have closed. Hispanic males, who historically have been among the lowest-performing student groups academically at Odessa, now complete an average of 96 percent of the classes they start, attain a grade of C or better in 78 percent of those classes, and, as a direct result of their improved classroom performance, have increased their graduation rate by more than 125 percent in the last five years.

Results such as these have catapulted Odessa College into the national discussion over how higher education can do more for more socioeconomically disadvantaged, underserved, and underrepresented students. The college was awarded the 2017 Aspen Prize Rising Star Award—America's signature recognition of high achievement and performance in the nation's community colleges.

Just five years earlier, however, in January 2011, Odessa College was one of four community colleges that were singled out—ultimately incorrectly and without grounds—by the Texas state legislature for possible defunding.

The path Odessa College has taken over the past several years to become the top-rated community college in the nation as determined by student success began with a single, unifying vision. The transformational processes and award-winning programs that have evolved from that vision are Odessa College's story. Our story includes administrators, faculty, and staff who have worked together in an "All In" spirit of change and transformation accomplished within existing budgets and without external grant funding. Accordingly, Odessa College's methods for improving student success are basically accessible to, and repeatable by, virtually any college.

CONTEXT: ODESSA COLLEGE AS IT WAS

Odessa College is located in the Permian Basin, one of the world's largest energy-producing regions, which provides almost one-third of all US oil and gas. Not surprisingly, the economy of the region has been dominated by the boom and bust cycles of the oil and gas industry. That industry also dominates college enrollments, which generally decline during full employment boom times and rise during busts as unemployment increases. Over the last few decades, the local population has increased; and in the 1970s, one more community college and one university were added to the region. Their presence further limited

Odessa College's enrollments, which, as the Texas legislature noted in its defunding announcement, hadn't changed in twenty years.

Along with enrollment/financial threats, Odessa's inattention to measuring student and institutional performance kept it at a standstill. Odessa College was a fairly typical rural community college focused on student access with little, if any, strategic planning around student success. The only student data of strong interest to college leadership was enrollment, because the state provided funding based on contact hours, which led to the only other data the college monitored and tracked for almost 60 years—revenue and expenses.

The college had not focused on student success and, indeed, had not measured determinants of student success such as classroom attendance or earning grades of C or better that would provide the necessary 2.0 grade point average needed to get a degree. Absent basic data about student performance, decisions by college leadership were mostly rooted in personal experience. In the classroom, "good teachers" were more often than not equated with individuals who had expertise in a particular subject area rather than on any measure of their effectiveness in improving academic outcomes. Indeed, the one piece of information that all instructors and instructional leadership had about student success—grades—was never analyzed from the perspective of using the data to make decisions about improving instruction and instructional effectiveness, but was instead simply used in anecdotal talking points for whether or not one year's class was better or worse than a previous year's class.

FIRST STEPS

In retrospect, three decisions—one by the college's board of trustees, the two others by the Odessa College (OC) administration—provided the necessary foundation for all that has followed. The trustees brought in Dr. Gregory Williams as the new president in 2007 with a mandate to improve student outcomes. Along with lack of focus on student success, Dr. Williams saw other signs that Odessa College was not moving forward. Buildings and grounds were old, classrooms were out-of-date, and, surprisingly, the college didn't actually have a front door for students.

There were no signs or other indications of where a student could go to register.

After many meetings, conferences, and discussions with the college's administration, the president was able to convince college leadership to join Achieving the Dream (AtD), a national nonprofit education-improvement organization founded in 2004 that champions evidence-based decision making as the preferred method for improving student success and achieving equity for minority and socioeconomic groups in community colleges. To further emphasize the commitment of college leadership to evidence-based decision making, the leadership decided to purchase a data-analytic software system before there was anyone on campus who knew how to use it. It came as a shock when the new system uncovered data showing that student success (C or better) and unduplicated graduation rates had been on a ten-year decline at Odessa College from 2000 through 2010, dropping by 7.5 percent and 6.5 percent respectively from their peaks.

Adopting Evidence-Based Decision Making

Student success came to the forefront for Odessa College leadership when they made two key decisions. The first was to fully embrace AtD's strategic objectives, including the use of evidence to improve policies, programs, and services to advance student success. A corollary to this decision was the objective of making sufficient improvements in student success to achieve Leader College status, AtD's highest honor for advancing student achievement.

The second decision of note was to compete for the Aspen Prize and measure progress against colleges that had achieved that distinction. The reasoning behind this decision was that even if the college never actually won the prize, the effort to achieve such a distinction would provide a unifying focus and common, easily understood objective around which all stakeholders could coordinate their efforts to improve student success.

With those decisions and the radically new strategic objectives they entailed, Odessa College began the process of redesigning its educational systems with the goal of improving student outcomes in four critical areas:

- Completion outcomes focused on helping students earn a degree with demonstrated value in the labor market and/or transfer to a four year college;
- Labor-market outcomes focused on improving employment and earnings of our graduates;
- Learning outcomes at both the course and program level to assess student learning and continually improve and strengthen courses and programs in accordance with those assessments; and
- Equitable outcomes to ensure both access and success for traditionally underserved students and those with socioeconomically disadvantaged backgrounds

Choosing Leading and Lagging Indicators

The beginning question was "Where to start?" in redesigning the college's educational system, which led to an important philosophical insight that has helped guide the college's path for improving student outcomes ever since: You can't teach them if they aren't there. We knew that we had to start with what we could control. Graduation rate improvement was out of the question; we could not make significant gains in this indicator quickly. We had to start with something that could get the entire college focused on "doing more to help more students."

This philosophy oriented college leadership to tackle two fundamental problems that had never before been addressed: (1) increasing college enrollment with programs that could overcome the historic enrollment ups and downs endemic to an economic environment dominated by a single industry and (2) increasing in-class retention. Both of these were leading indicators over which the college could exert some control. One of the challenges was the sheer number of indicators from which to choose. It was also necessary to keep in mind that instructors and staff could only work with data that were obviously relevant to their job-related objectives and the activities they oversaw to meet those objectives.

With the above in mind, it was clear that the two strategic goals of enrolling more students and keeping them in class were controlled by two different areas: student services for enrolling more students and instruction for keeping them in class. Without success in both areas, lagging indicators such as credit attainment required for progress in advancing toward a degree and graduation rate improvement demonstrating successful degree attainment could never change substantially.

Both student services and instruction, however, faced the same undeniable challenge: they had to considerably change processes, procedures, and even perspective on what would they could do to improve student success. Historically, the ways those operations had been structured and organized to accomplish—through job descriptions, roles, and responsibilities—and what staff had been rewarded for with raises and praises for more than six decades had done little to advance enrollment and even less to improve student achievement and degree attainment.

Transformational change had to occur at every level—from supervisor and department chair to staff and instructor; from roles and responsibilities affecting senior staff and new hires to accountability based on effectiveness and not years of service. As with most colleges attempting such big change, however, the barriers posed by status quo inertia loomed large and an operational culture that reinforced a "that's how we have always done it" mentality provided automatic day-to-day resistance throughout the college.

THE DROP RATE IMPROVEMENT PROGRAM

Ironically, the spark that lit the accelerant for a new direction led by evidence-based change to the status quo and the beginnings of a significant change in the operational culture was the 2011 possible defunding announcement by the Texas legislature. At about the same time, Dr. Donald Wood, newly appointed as associate dean of Arts and Sciences who had been learning how to use the new analytic software approached Dr. Williams with data suggesting that student dropouts from class (a leading indicator), which were averaging close to 20 percent for all college enrollments, appeared to correlate much more with the instructor teaching the course than with anything else. (The dropout rate is the percentage of students on census day who withdraw from or drop a class for whatever reason on or before the last day to withdraw.) Moreover, instructors with low student dropout rates appeared to share four activities in common (addressing students by name, monitoring and quickly addressing student behavior, meeting one-on-one with students, and establishing clear expectations) that improved the student-instructor connection and kept students in class. Those instructors with high dropout rates might do one or two, but never all of those four activities.

From this data, Odessa College's award-winning Drop Rate Improvement Program was created; and from the urgency brought by the defunding scare the program was introduced to the faculty in late spring 2011 and put in place in fall 2011. Results were dramatic and immediate.[1] Every single instructor with high drop rates (over 17 percent) improved, mostly to single-digit drop rates that most had never experienced in their entire career. Indeed the entire Arts and Sciences division class dropout rate overall, which had averaged over 14 percent for the previous ten years, fell to 9.6 percent—the lowest in history—in that first semester. That success has continued, and the class dropout rate for students in Arts and Sciences in the most recent fall 2016 semester was a record low of 3.2 percent. The rate for the entire college—all students, all classes, and all instructors—was 3.0 percent.

The four tenets of the Drop Rate Improvement Program focus on strengthening the connection between instructor and student by having the instructor actively engage in the following behaviors:

1. **Interact with each student by name from the first day of class.**
   Instructors at Odessa College use the first day of class getting to know their students and letting their students know who they are as well.
2. **Monitor student behavior and intervene immediately if anything should appear amiss.** In practice, there are hundreds of anecdotes about what instructors do if students come late to class, fall asleep in class, fail their first exam or pop quiz, etc. The only common point is that they do something that is appropriate in the circumstance and reinforces to the students that they do care, they are watching them, and they will look for ways to help them succeed.
3. **Meet one-on-one with the student sometime early in the semester.** Such meetings need not be extensive, but there must be a moment when there is a personal connection between instructor and

student. In these individual meetings, students are made aware that the instructor is glad to have them in the class and looks forward to working to help them to succeed.

4. Establish clear expectations as set forth in an extensive and comprehensive syllabus that lays out logical penalties for missed exams, late assignments, etc., but also acknowledges the instructor's willingness to be flexible when appropriate.

A surprise outcome noticed in the first semester of the Drop Rate Improvement Program was that the percentage of students on census day who completed their class with a grade of C or better increased dramatically from the fall semester one year earlier (see table 9.1).

Student drops in the fall 2010 semester in the Arts and Sciences program averaged 14 percent, and student success averaged 56.7 percent.

TABLE 9.1   Significant decreases in drop rates and increases in success rates associated with implementation of the Drop Rate Improvement Program

| | Before Drop Rate Improvement Program | | | First semester of Drop Rate Improvement Program | | | Five years of Drop Rate Improvement Program, | | |
| | Fall 2010 | | | Fall 2011 | | | Fall 2016 | | |
	Drop	Success	Enrollment	Drop	Success	Enrollment	Drop	Success	Enrollment
All	12.5%	69.8%	12,318	9.3%	72.8%	12,799	2.0%	80.6%	14,079
Female	12.2%	71.9%	7,414	9.2%	75.2%	8,070	2.0%	81.2%	8,338
Male	13.1%	66.6%	4,944	9.4%	68.5%	4,729	2.0%	79.6%	5,741
Hispanic	12.6%	68.6%	6,490	9.2%	71.1%	7,107	2.0%	80.0%	8,508
White	13.1%	72.5%	5,049	9.3%	75.7%	4,957	1.9%	82.9%	4,120
African American	13.6%	57.6%	583	11.1%	61.5%	478	2.7%	73.0%	777
Pell	11.7%	70.5%	6,813	9.1%	73.4%	7,193	1.8%	79.8%	6,647
Non-Pell	13.2%	69.1%	5,525	9.5%	72.0%	5,606	2.2%	81.2%	7,432

Under the Drop Rate Improvement Program, with no changes in student learning outcomes or instructor pedagogy, the fall 2011 student success rates rose to 64.4 percent, a 7.7 percent absolute increase in student success outcomes in classes taught for the most part by the same instructors who had taught those classes a year earlier. As with steady improvements in the drop rates over the past five years, student success rates have also continued to improve and for the entire college reached 80.8 percent in the fall 2016 semester.

The early and immediate positive results on student outcomes with initiation of the Drop Rate Improvement Program led to a newfound appreciation among college leadership about the importance of focusing on leading indicators like classroom attendance as well as on things that could actually be controlled through intentional effort and action. It was also surprising to most faculty that not only did students stay in class at unprecedented levels when they—the instructors—faithfully executed the four tenets of the Drop Rate Improvement Program, but that students studied more, did better on assignments, and succeeded at ever higher levels when the connection between instructor and student was strengthened. And this was true for key subpopulations of interest: first-time-in-college (FTIC) students, socioeconomically disadvantaged (Pell grant–supported) students, and others (table 9.2).

The transformation in student behavior—improved class completion and success (i.e., as obtaining a C grade or better)—during the first semester the Drop Rate Improvement Program was implemented was eye-opening for college leadership. A literature review did not reveal any previous case study or research-based report in which a college transformed the in-class completion behavior and grade outcomes of an entire student body in one semester using an approach that did not add cost to the college budget, require a change in pedagogy, or impact academic freedom. As college leaders, we realized that in the Drop Rate Improvement Program, we had a potentially game-changing approach for improving student success in virtually every classroom, every department, and every division of the college. But the linked issues of how to sustain such improvement on the one hand and, on the other, how to build on the success of that first semester arose almost immediately.

TABLE 9.2   Face-to-face classes: Significant improvement in success rates after initiating Drop Rate Improvement Program*

| | Before Drop Rate Improvement Program | | | First semester of Drop Rate Improvement Program | | | Five years of Drop Rate Improvement Program | | |
| | Fall 2010 | | | Fall 2011 | | | Fall 2016 | | |
	Drop	Success	Enrollment	Drop	Success	Enrollment	Drop	Success	Enrollment
All	11.8%	71.7%	7,210	8.1%	75.8%	7,038	1.5%	83.5%	7,987
Female	10.6%	75.4%	4,266	8.2%	79.2%	4,357	1.5%	84.4%	4,558
Male	13.5%	66.4%	2,944	8.1%	70.3%	2,681	1.5%	82.3%	3,429
Hispanic	11.3%	71.4%	3,929	8.1%	74.6%	4,144	1.6%	83.0%	5,177
White	12.4%	73.5%	2,817	8.1%	78.1%	2,505	1.3%	85.1%	1,995
African American	13.0%	59.3%	324	11.6%	67.2%	241	2.0%	75.4%	411
Pell	10.4%	73.7%	3,974	8.1%	75.8%	3,895	1.2%	83.5%	3,580
Non-Pell	13.4%	69.3%	3,236	8.3%	73.9%	3,143	1.7%	83.5%	4,407

*All courses except dual credit and developmental education.

The answers to both questions emerged over the next few semesters as we strengthened our infrastructure for evidence-based decision making and brought leading indicator data to the forefront of both instruction and student services, where job one at the college became improving the leading indicators: college enrollment, in-class completion, and student success. Longitudinal data for these three leading indicators provided comparisons from before to after programs, initiatives, and new directions were initiated. This data was intentionally and frequently shared with all stakeholders. For example, success was shared at all monthly board meetings and at twice-monthly "Coffee and Conversations" for faculty and staff. So everyone was aware of the data and, importantly, could take part in celebrating advances and accomplishments.

INSTITUTIONALIZING EVIDENCE-BASED DECISION MAKING

With the knowledge and experience gained from participating in the AtD initiative along with the impetus and sense of urgency created by the defunding scare and the undeniable success of the Drop Rate Improvement Program, Odessa College leadership made several moves early in 2012 to institutionalize evidence-based decision making.

First, data on student success, progress on initiatives to improve student success, and related subjects was discussed at all board of trustee meetings. Second, college leadership next established a new Vice President for Institutional Effectiveness position and expanded resources for that department to strengthen and enhance data-driven decision making at all levels of the college and to foster a data-driven culture leading to continuous improvement in student success. Third, the Vice President for Institutional Effectiveness, Dr. Donald Wood, was made an equal member of the president's administrative team that meets weekly to review, among other things, student success data and to make data-driven decisions on resources required to improve student success. Fourth, strategic planning for the college was reorganized to align all areas of the college in supporting two key strategic lagging indicators: improving completion outcomes and educational attainment objectives by more students and building enrollment in both oil boom and bust times. Quantifiable and measurable objectives for these indicators were established at the start of each year and appropriate evidence-based decisions made for what changes and actions were needed within the existing budget to meet those goals.

Finally, daily enrollment and payment information metrics compared with those for the same time in the previous year were introduced so that college leaders, marketing, enrollment management, and financial accounts personnel knew exactly how many students were enrolled for the upcoming semesters and whether the trend was up or down. The up-to-the minute information on current enrollment and trends led to numerous new initiatives in marketing and proactive efforts by enrollment management and financial staff to contact students and find ways to help them enroll for the first time or re-enroll. Cumulatively, these data-driven, proactive efforts have led to record enrollments and con-tinuous growth for the past several years.

Odessa College institutionalized evidence-based decision making using a robust strategic planning and budgeting process. Weekly meetings of college leadership to review progress and ensure agreed-upon indica-tors were being addressed, as well as daily information on enrollments, empowered all stakeholders, including faculty, staff, and administra-tors, to participate in the effort to transform the college-going, college-completing culture of our students by sharing data, fostering leadership, and learning from experience. Data, leadership, and experience drive the student-focused programs at the college and have helped to create an environment where stakeholders at all levels look for answers to one question: *How can we do more to help our students?* Seeking answers to this question has led to implementing a number of innovations.

First, the college transitioned instruction and advising to eight-week terms from the traditional sixteen-week course schedule, which is per-haps the most dramatic new approach to higher education taken by Odessa College. This was an unprecedented change in the history of Texas higher education, requiring support from the Texas Higher Educa-tion Coordinating Board. Benefits included:

- Unduplicated student enrollment up 17.4 percent and 6,186 unduplicated students in fall 2016, versus the sixteen-week record of 5,268 in fall 2010
- Student success up to 80.6 percent (students present on census day who finish the course with a grade of C or better) for the most recent eight-week fall 2016 semester, as compared with 74.5 percent in fall 2013, which was the highest level achieved under the sixteen-week course format

Second, the Strategies for Success course is a reinvented, mandatory one-credit-hour college preparatory course for all FTIC students. It offers two foundational college experience enhancements: an AVID-based tool kit for building a successful college experience and career planning and exploration. AVID (Advancement Via Individual Determination) uses an inquiry-based engagement strategy to assist students to assume respon-sibility for themselves as learners. The foundation of AVID's approach to improve student learning is a basic tool kit that helps students develop and improve their skills in writing, inquiry, collaboration, organization, and reading. In 2016, Odessa College was selected as AVID's first higher education demonstration site. Along with the transition to eight-week courses, benefits have included:

- FTIC unduplicated student enrollment up 21.1 percent; 1,047 FTIC students in fall 2016 over the sixteen-week record of 864 unduplicated students in fall 2010
- FTIC student dropout down from 13.7 percent in fall 2010 to 2.8 percent in fall 2016
- FTIC student success up from 61.8 percent in fall 2010 to 77.4 percent in fall 2016

Table 9.3 summarizes these findings, with emphasis on the reduction in drop rate.

TABLE 9.3   First-time-In-college students greatly reduced their drop rates after implementation of the Drop Rate Improvement Program

	Before Drop Rate Improvement Program			First semester of Drop Rate Improvement Program			Five years of Drop Rate Improvement Program		
	Fall 2010			*Fall 2011*			*Fall 2016*		
	Drop	Success	Enrollment	Drop	Success	Enrollment	Drop	Success	Enrollment
All	13.7%	61.8%	2,494	9.9%	64.8%	2,713	2.8%	77.4%	3,810
Female	11.6%	66.8%	1,360	8.7%	68.2%	1,548	2.1%	80.8%	2,017
Male	16.1%	55.8%	1,134	11.5%	60.3%	1,165	3.6%	73.6%	1,793
Hispanic	11.5%	62.5%	1,362	9.1%	64.1%	1,592	2.8%	77.0%	2,467
White	16.8%	61.7%	993	11.8%	64.5%	960	3.1%	77.0%	957
African American	16.1%	55.9%	93	8.5%	70.9%	141	4.1%	74.3%	197
Pell	10.4%	64.4%	1,305	8.9%	65.3%	1,508	2.7%	75.3%	1,633
Non-Pell	17.3%	58.9%	1,189	11.2%	64.2%	1,205	2.9%	79.0%	2,177

Third, the college implemented a Student Success Coach program that reimagined advising with a holistic team approach and individual wraparound support for all students from their first day on campus until transfer or graduation. With an emphasis on college completion and career planning, this program provides each student with a Student Success Coach to explore career options, a faculty adviser from the student's career interest area, and a faculty mentor. Meetings with coaches and advisers each term are mandatory. Some of the outcomes of this program have included:

- A 98 percent increase in unduplicated students obtaining a degree, from 515 in academic year (AY) 2009 to 1,021 in AY 2015, and a 160 percent increase in degrees awarded from 608 in AY 2009 to 1,313 in AY 2015.
- The highest first-year earnings by community college graduates in the region, at an average of $46,884, which is 11.6 percent greater than the second-highest community college in the region and 39.3 percent greater than the Texas state average for community college graduates.[2]

The success resulting from tracking student dropout rates and student success rates created a buzz among the faculty and staff. Everyone was focused on how much improvement could be made. More and more stakeholders became aware of the transformation in student outcomes. What was unusual, however, was that the very nature of the Drop Rate Improvement Program led to tracking those outcomes by instructor. An issue arose early in the program over what the implications should be if an instructor's student drops increased rather than decreased from one semester to the next. Over the five years the program has been in place, Odessa College has learned that student dropout rates are far and away the most sensitive indicator that something is not going right in the classroom. Pinpointing the problem is the first critically important step in helping instructors gain insight into what can be done to reduce dropouts from their classes. The second step is developing an action plan to reduce the drops.

Data on student withdrawals from class and student success also began to uncover very specific areas in need of improvement; for example, dropout rates were higher and student success rates lower in online courses than in face-to-face classes. However, the data also revealed areas of strength that had not previously been recognized. Some instructors were absolutely amazing in their ability to connect with students, as revealed by their low dropout rates and high success rates—and they quickly became champions, encouraging others to try new ways to connect with students. As the evidence grew that improving the connection between instructors and students through instructor-initiated actions led to immediate improvement in student success, it became imperative to institutionalize the program so that it could be repeated with fidelity with every new instructor and in every course.

Accordingly, a new Dean of Teaching and Learning position was created with the mandate to oversee faculty mentoring, professional development, and related support systems that have as their goal improving the connection between instructor and student as measured by student drop and success rates. The success of this focus on improving the student-instructor connection can be seen in the most recent spring 2016 semester, where over 40 percent of full-time and adjunct faculty had no student dropouts from classes they taught—including online sections— and success rates averaged greater than 80 percent for the entire college.

EMERGING INSIGHTS

Over the past five years, evidence-based decision making has become a routine part of the Odessa College culture. Additionally, all stakeholders are aware of, and celebrate, progress in student enrollment and educational attainment: the two North Stars of the college's strategic direction. An important outcome of this culture is that new insights related to areas of opportunity to improve student outcomes are emerging. One powerful example comes from student performance in face-to-face classes in comparison to their performance in online classes. Table 9.2 (above) shows the dramatic improvement in student outcomes that has occurred over the past five years in face-to-face classes, where success rates have risen eleven to sixteen percentage points and now average over 82 percent with minimal to no gaps between different socioeconomic student groups, genders, and ethnic groups.

The data for students in online courses (table 9.4), however, throws a spotlight on where there is still work to do. Although the trend for all disaggregated student groups is toward lower dropouts and higher success, there are still significant achievement gaps between the different ethnicities, and success rates for all student groups remain below those for students in face-to-face classes.

TABLE 9.4   Online classes: Significant improvement in success rates after initiating Drop Rate Improvement Program*

	Before Drop Rate Improvement Program			First semester of Drop Rate Improvement Program			Five years of Drop Rate Improvement Program,		
	Fall 2010			Fall 2011			Fall 2016		
	Drop	Success	Enrollment	Drop	Success	Enrollment	Drop	Success	Enrollment
All	15.0%	61.6%	3,397	12.0%	64.1%	4,268	5.5%	72.2%	5,448
Female	15.4%	62.2%	2,133	11.3%	66.5%	2,802	5.5%	73.2%	3,467
Male	14.4%	60.6%	1,264	13.2%	59.6%	1,466	3.6%	73.6%	1,793
Hispanic	15.5%	57.9%	1,634	12.2%	60.3%	2,196	5.4%	70.0%	3,024
White	14.5%	67.2%	1,535	11.8%	69.7%	1,834	5.8%	76.2%	1,890
African American	16.9%	45.6%	160	13.7%	47.0%	168	7.4%	63.8%	326
Pell	15.3%	61.2%	1,918	11.5%	64.1%	2,490	5.1%	71.7%	2,824
Non-Pell	14.7%	62.1%	1,479	12.6%	64.2%	1,778	6.0%	72.8%	2,624

*All courses except dual credit and developmental education.

TRANSFORMING EMPLOYEE BEHAVIOR

Odessa College's story in transforming the college-going and college-completing behavior of our students over the past five years, leading to the attainment of historic highs in both leading and lagging indicators, certainly includes the introduction of and immediate collegewide scale-up of dramatically effective new programs, such as the Drop Rate Improvement Program and the transition from sixteen-week to eight-week courses. But for colleges interested in replicating such transformative behavior in their students, it's important to emphasize that the widespread positive impact and growing success of Odessa College's programs across all student subpopulations has emerged from, and is sustained by, employee-focused programs oriented toward building, strengthening, and expanding a shared vision and common bond among all Odessa College stakeholders and employees. The vision is that no matter their job, no matter their length of employment, no matter their status as administrator, instructor, or staff, each employee is here to serve our students, to better our community, and to support his or her colleagues as a valued member of the Odessa College team—a team that is student-centered and focused on becoming the top community college in the nation for improving student success.

The underlying principle driving the effort is having employees join together in common cause with shared accountability for improving student success. Even before introduction of student-focused programs such as the Drop Rate Improvement Program, employees understood that a change in student behavior that leads to greater academic achievement could not occur without a change in college employees' behavior. That change contributes in positive ways both directly and indirectly toward student success.

Odessa College's president, Dr. Williams, took the lead in bringing together staff, faculty, and the administrative team in common cause by instituting events and activities designed to improve communications among and between all stakeholders. He modeled total transparency about college successes, challenges, goals, and achievements. The president and the administrative team took every opportunity to reinforce the concept that when it came to student achievement, the college's strategic direction was oriented not only toward becoming the number-one community college in the nation but was counting on—indeed, expecting—each department and division of the college to take on the same challenge for themselves: to become the very best in the nation at what they did.

Odessa College instituted expanded communication and transparency forums that involve administration, instructors, and staff in equitably shared activities that took a number of forms. The Coffee and Conversation forums mentioned above are twice-monthly one-hour meetings that include fifteen minutes of socializing over coffee and pastries, a thirty-minute presentation by a department of the college on initiatives and progress in improving their area, and fifteen minutes with the president and administrative team where anyone is allowed, and everyone is encouraged, to ask questions about what the college is planning and doing: from raises and budgets to hiring and performance evaluations. Anything and everything is open for discussion.

Second, there are "Birthday Bashes": once-monthly get-together celebrations with refreshments for everyone at the college, with a drawing for those who had birthdays during the preceding month to win $25 gift certificates to local restaurants and a $100 grand prize. The president or a member of the administrative team oversees the drawing, and there is considerable socializing among instructors and staff.

Third, the college implemented once-monthly meetings of the administrative team (president, and vice presidents for instruction, student services, business affairs, information technology, and institutional effectiveness) and *all* their direct reports to discuss progress on major initiatives, brainstorm new initiatives, review major strategic goals, and more. This provides continuous transparency of all major college activities to all department heads.

Another important aspect of employee performance is participation in voluntary events such as Phi Theta Kappa inductions, sporting events, student plays, concerts, and art exhibits. Participation also is encouraged for attendance at important college activities such as board of trustees meetings, student scholarship award ceremonies, and media events such as check presentations from corporate sponsors. Odessa College's transformative program in this area is the OC All-In program instituted in 2015.

OC All-In is a voluntary program in which all full-time employees, including the president, the administrative team, faculty, and staff, earn points by attending the events described above. An OC All-In app allows an employee to check in at an event and, by entering a random four-digit code that is revealed only at the event, to keep track of the cumulative points earned per eight-week term. When an employee hits the OC All-In point total threshold representing his or her participation in a minimum number of events for that term, the employee receives a $25 gift certificate at a celebration event held each term that brings together all employees who achieved the threshold.

At the beginning of the academic year, the college establishes four leading indicator goals; for example, FTIC student enrollment, overall enrollment, student success in the classroom, etc. If the college achieves all four goals, then all employees can win an additional $100.

The OC All-In program has transformed attendance levels at college events; some now drawing upward of 85 percent of all full-time employees. In the aggregate, almost 98 percent of all employees participate in the program during the course of the year. The benefits of this program have been incalculable in terms of team building and creating the very real feeling that at Odessa College, we are all in this effort together.

TRANSFORMING A COMMUNITY COLLEGE

A number of factors can make community college leadership very challenging. One of these factors is culture. Historically, the prevailing culture at many community colleges has been to manage operations from a collective experience perspective where anecdotal evidence about best practices and common sense solutions about what should and shouldn't work formed the foundational touchstones for decision making. At Odessa, leadership modeled using student outcome data to inform decision making. An additional challenge for community colleges is that they have functioned for many years with a very uneven level of accountability among campus employees. Historically, poor performance at the administrative and staff level has generally led to corrective actions. There has, however, been a long-standing caution about approaching faculty in the same manner. In part, this is because there has been no agreed-upon performance metric by which to measure instructional effectiveness.

At Odessa College, however, the objective science underlying the Drop Rate Improvement Program, along with the extraordinary outcomes in student in-class retention and success the faculty have achieved by adhering to the program, have opened the door for a new dialogue centered on student outcomes. Using student dropouts and success as appropriate metrics for instructor effectiveness in applying the tenets of the Drop Rate Improvement Program, an agreed upon level of instructor accountability has been established. With it has come a new culture of equitably shared cooperation among all stakeholders to improve student success.

Shared cooperation means that all Odessa College employees, starting with the president, must be held accountable for the college's success and the success of the students we serve. Accordingly, we believe that every function of the college needs to have a number, or indicator, so that everyone can recognize what works and what doesn't work. Quality performance indicators such as daily enrollment numbers allow us to monitor outcomes and improve the institution in a continuous manner.

At Odessa, we attempt to give our students every chance for academic, social, and financial success. This means that every operating unit of the college—instruction, student services, business affairs, information technology, institutional effectiveness, and institutional advancement—must have leading indicators that can be measured and that directly or indirectly contribute to our lagging indicators of increased enrollment and/or improved educational attainment by our students. It was through the lens of this perspective that college leadership was able and willing to take advantage of the Drop Rate Improvement Program when it was first presented.

In a system that generally functions with limited financial resources, our goal is to take advantage of all available resources to maximize effectiveness. Each institution will have a different set of challenges and opportunities. At Odessa College, we set our first standards of excellence by benchmarking against the most outstanding colleges in our state and in the nation. Those indicators grow, therefore, in concert with those colleges that are most effective in improving student outcomes. With the expectation of excellence as a part of our culture, tough decisions become easier to make. Every person, program, or purchase must make a contribution to making the college better. This is the Odessa College way.

A final note to community college leaders: The Odessa College journey has shown that community college leaders should also work to
include their boards as they seek to improve student learning outcomes.
Boards are often left out of the college performance and accountability conversations. That is not an effective approach. When boards are
included on the front end, when key decisions are being made, it then
becomes much easier to gain their support when and if conflicts occur.

Embracing a New Data Use Paradigm

In this book, we present a model for data use in support of student success that can be applied at any college. The three components of the model—analytics, human judgment and decision making, and organizational habits—are designed to reform what data is examined, how it is presented, and how it is used. We go beyond data literacy and move the focus to the interactions between data, people, and colleges. The drivers of this work are leading and lagging indicators. We also present information about widely experienced student success issues and how to select high-impact, research-based solutions to address them. To illustrate the impact of using the model, we presented three case studies authored by college leaders who have used the model to make major changes.

FIVE BIG IDEAS

Let's revisit some of the big ideas from the book. First, a key to changing the paradigm to increase data use is that an institution has to decide to focus. We have emphasized this throughout this text. Without focus, nothing will change, because in an institution, there are not enough resources to address everything that we would like to address. This is a fundamental principle that has to be accepted if we are to change how we approach increasing data use. Along with focusing efforts, it is essential to keep the number of indicators examined manageable. Institutional researchers have to be good gatekeepers. While this is a difficult ask, it is important that they analyze data deeply only in areas that are required by reporting mandates or support-and-inform decisions about changes to policy and practice.

Second, educators need to think about what they are doing in the context of changing students' lives and helping them to earn a living wage to support themselves and their families. Without the passion to make a difference, educators will only go through the motions. Remember, human beings like things to remain the same. Unless we tap into their passion—and hopefully, that passion is to increase student success—we will not get the kind of buy-in needed to address the data that's important and move toward making changes to solve real problems that our students are facing.

Third, we have presented many techniques for maximizing the understanding of data. These techniques have been honed and practiced at a number of community colleges around the country. They work well. In our experience, increased understanding of the data leads to the conversations that can move an institution forward to action— implementing aligned policies and practices that address the problems the institution is trying to solve. The bottom line is that these techniques help to enhance human judgment and good decision making.

Fourth, when it comes to metrics, we strongly recommend that a college avoid the temptation to analyze only lagging indicators, such as graduation and transfer rates. Colleges must look to the roots of those indicators: leading indicators, such as class retention and class success, that contribute to these desired outcomes. If students are not retained in class and are not successful, they likely do not persist, they certainly do not earn credits, and, of course, they do not achieve their education goals. This means we have to include the faculty and staff and gain their expertise, insight, and especially their support in monitoring these metrics.

Finally, we have to disaggregate data to ensure that students from various groups are achieving at roughly the same high levels. Subpopulation breakouts are not just between the common demographic areas, but also between socioeconomic groups, first-time-in-college students, and various other groups such as veterans, foster youth, day and evening students, and disabled students.

CHALLENGES TO MOVING FORWARD

We know that colleges can run into difficulties implementing our recommendations. Let's address some of the common challenges in increasing data use.

Funding. Unfortunately, funding for community colleges is not stable. It varies from year to year, and at times it feels like we are on a roller coaster. Fortunately, increasing data use is not expensive. In fact, we believe little to no monetary resources need to be reallocated to support it, and that the paradigm shift we are suggesting might even save money. This is because we are not necessarily advocating for the latest and greatest software on the market. We are not saying don't buy the software. We are saying don't expect the software that can generate hundreds and hundreds of tables and charts, that can slice and dice data in a myriad of ways, and predict student behavior to be embraced by the college community. In our experience, there is the rare power user who will dive into the software to do great things. IR staff can definitely benefit from the software, but the expectation to have the software on everyone's desktop answering questions on the fly, as needed, has not come to fruition and likely won't.

Lack of Focus. Some states and institutions we have worked with can have what we call an "issue of the week" problem. This is what is known as a "new shiny penny" mentality. They bounce around from issue to issue or from practice to practice, expecting the silver bullet that changes student outcomes. Unfortunately, there is very little that we have seen where attempts to improve student success can be actualized without a deep and sustained focus. Even worse is that most institutions facing this quandary pay lip service to a mandate or to the new area of interest and do not fully engage in addressing it. In fact, this kind of jumping from one issue to another reinforces stasis at the institution.

We advocate for institutions to examine their own data in their own culture and to determine which of the few problem areas that rise to the top need to be addressed. And to identify them, a college uses both quantitative and qualitative data, to fully analyze the issue at hand to understand not only what is going on but why it may be occurring. Only after an institution begins to address its problems using leading indicators, can it become truly committed to monitoring the policy and/or practice implementation and outcomes to ensure that the intervention made a difference.

Leadership Changes. Leadership changes are one of the most difficult challenges when addressing student success; not only for increasing data use but for many areas related to making and sustaining change. However, increasing data use does not have to begin with the CEO, although that is preferable because when he or she becomes the data champion, change happens. IR directors, vice presidents, deans, and faculty can begin to make the changes we suggest immediately. Our experience has been that once a college community begins to see how data can be presented and digested, courageous conversations occur. As a result of this work, the culture of the institution changes, even if the initiative is not fostered by the CEO. Using data well is really about habit change. In order for habits to change, the change efforts must be grounded in modifying existing practices; and new behaviors must be practiced enough so that they are locked in and have become part of the fabric of the everyday activities of the college.

Resistance to Change. Resistance to change is one of the most insidious problems a college has to deal with when implementing new ways of using data to aid student success. Human beings like to keep things the same. That thinking can result in resistance to better ways of using data in the form of comments such as "I'm not used to seeing data in this way" or "How come we are looking at this data?" In our experience, when the data is shared using the methods we suggest—such as focusing on a key simple indicator, putting the message in the chart title, and using templates—most educators greatly appreciate this new approach.

We have, however, come across educators who have dug in their heels and wanted to continue seeing "their" data. In those cases, we suggest they continue to do so while the rest of the group moves on ahead of them.

REFLECTING ON THE CASE STUDIES

The three case studies presented in chapters 7, 8, and 9 exemplify much of what we have laid out in this book and reflect the strategies and techniques we have been espousing. In chapter 7, Lauren Sosenko, Director of Institutional Research at Long Beach City College (LBCC), demonstrates how quickly and easily skilled use of the model can make dramatic changes in the perception and use of institutional research data for strategic planning. Sosenko had the advantage of being a former IEBC staff member. At IEBC, she was exposed to and helped implement parts of our data-use model. As her account shows, the change in attitude at LBCC about data use was immediate. Focusing on leading and lagging indicators, the SPOT team had courageous conversations around the data and began drilling down into it. Data was presented in such a way that faculty and staff finally understood the numbers. In personal conversations with us, Sosenko relayed comments from the faculty and staff such as "I finally get this stuff!" Presenting data in simple, easy-to-understand formats—where she did the analysis, rather than expecting it to be done by LBCC educators—enabled faculty to have conversations right away. Faculty and staff were grateful for her help in supporting their work.

LBCC, while still in the early stages of its planning agenda, has made great strides in developing the right indicators to understand how leading and lagging indicators relate to one another, and how leading indicators in a specific area relate to the overall lagging indicators. The college has begun to integrate tools such as Tableau and Civitas into the IR function to support increased data use.

In chapter 8, Angelica Suarez, Vice President for Student Affairs at Southwestern College (SWC), recounts how SWC employed IEBC's data use model to address a particular issue: student equity. In this work, aspects of the data-use model were used to shift from the typical paradigm of looking at a lot of data and trying to figure out what it meant to focusing on the data that mattered most, ensuring that interventions aligned with the agreed-upon problems the student success committee was trying to solve.

SWC took a deep dive into the data on student equity outcomes and made certain that committee members charged with determining where resources should be spent fully understood the data—and most importantly, set criteria for what interventions could be considered in their attempt to improve student outcomes in a meaningful way. Using criteria to determine the appropriateness of an intervention was something that SWC had never done before.

The results of SWC's interventions are encouraging. One powerful proof is that the process that the committee engaged in to address a particular problem by deeply understanding student outcomes and then aligning the appropriate intervention with those outcomes is now moving into other areas of the college.

Chapter 9, authored by Gregory D. Williams, President of Odessa College, and Don Wood, its Vice President for Institutional Effectiveness, describes the college's transformation through data use. The change effort focused exclusively on leading and lagging indicators. The degree of focus the leadership team had and the discipline they exerted to keep this focus is one of the reasons the college is now an Aspen top-10 award winner and was the 2017 Aspen Rising Star award recipient. The leadership team focused almost exclusively on course retention data. This set them on a path to do a deep dive, examining not only course retention across the entire institution but also looking at breakouts from the traditional indicators of race/ethnicity, age, gender, and socioeconomic status, to the time of day a course was taught, to the type of course itself.

This deep dive engaged the entire college community, and the habits they created around focusing on leading indicators has truly changed Odessa College's culture. The college also instituted a habit of trying different things without holding people accountable in a negative way if the intervention fails. It is truly a culture that creates a laboratory of experimentation around doing what matters, while allowing for all-too-human mistakes, in the effort to improve student outcomes.

■ ■ ■

While these three case studies have not fully embraced everything we have discussed in this book, it's important to note that not all of the processes and techniques we describe have to be implemented to make change. That is, as we said earlier, in order to change culture, behavior has to change. These behaviors can and do increase the use of data.

SOME ADDITIONAL THOUGHTS

Our work with community colleges gives us hope. While not every college we worked with fully embraces the changes we described, they often take baby steps toward increasing data use. We have found that two or three years after we have had an engagement with the college, much of what we talked about actually sticks.

For example, during the time of writing this chapter, we learned that a college we had worked with on focusing had finally decided to really focus. When we arrived, the college had over two hundred metrics, each of which was important to someone in the institution. During our workshop, there was great resistance to giving up many of these metrics, which the college had spent years developing. They recently invited us back to help them do a deep dive into the *four* metrics that they had decided to keep! It took them about a year of deliberation after the workshop to finally agree to focus on these four metrics. Now they are ready to fully engage with the college community on these metrics.

Community college educators nationwide have big hearts and want to make a difference by improving student outcomes in support of the students who seek them out. But change is hard, and breaking old patterns of behavior is difficult. It takes courage to embrace this new data-use paradigm and move forward in a different way.

As we have emphasized throughout this book, this new model, grounded in neuroscience, behavioral economics and psychology, really does work. So now it's time to get started. We recommend that a college begin by focusing on a very limited set of indicators.

CLOSING REMARKS

While there is much work to do in improving student outcomes at community colleges, we live by the expression "If you're not having fun, you're not getting it done." This work should not be onerous. Learning about and supporting students is interesting and exciting work. Our hope is that community college educators agree with us and are ready to begin the journey of working to improve student outcomes through increasing their use of data—and to have fun doing it.

Community colleges face tremendous challenges and also have extraordinary opportunities. We know our nation's community colleges are up to the task.

Introduction

1. National Center for Education Statistics. *Condition of Education: Characteristics of Postsecondary Students*. (Washington, DC: Institute of Education Sciences, 2016).
2. Jolanta Juszkiewicz. *Trends in Community College Enrollment and Completion Data* (Washington, DC: American Association of Community Colleges, 2016).
3. State Higher Education Executive Officers Association. *State Higher Education Finance: FY2014* (Boulder, CO: State Higher Education Executive Officers Association, 2015).
4. Achieving the Dream, 2016, https://youtu.be/XWa2wu1Is6Q.
5. Juszkiewicz. *Trends in Community College Enrollment and Completion Data.*
6. Marie Bienkowski, Mingyu Feng, and Barbara Means, *Enhancing Teaching and Learning Through Educational Data Mining and Learning Analytics: An Issue Brief* (Washington, DC: US Department of Education, 2012).
7. Chip Heath and Dan Heath, *Made to Stick: Why Some Ideas Survive and Others Die* (New York: Random House, 2007).
8. Charles Duhigg, *The Power of Habit: Why We Do What We Do in Life and Business* (New York: Random House, 2014).

Chapter 1

1. Mario Morino, "We're Lost But Making Good Time," in *Leap of Reason: Managing to Outcomes in an Era of Scarcity*, ed. M. Morino (Washington, DC: Venture Philanthropy Partners, 2011), 1–11.
2. Chip Heath and Dan Heath, *Switch: How to Change Things When Change Is Hard* (New York: Random House, 2010).
3. http://www.dictionary.com/browse/analytics?s=t.
4. Elizabeth Kübler-Ross, *On Death and Dying* (New York: Macmillan, 1969).
5. Centers for Disease Control, *Behavior Risk Factor Surveillance System (BRFSS), 2003–2014* (Washington, DC: US Department of Health and Human Services, 2015).
6. Floyd J. Fowler, Jr., *Improving Survey Questions: Design and Evaluation*, Applied Social Research Methods Series, vol. 38 (Thousand Oaks, CA: Sage, 1995).

7. Marie Bienkowski, Mingyu Feng, and Barbara Means, *Enhancing Teaching and Learning Through Educational Data Mining and Learning Analytics: An Issue Brief* (Washington, DC: US Department of Education, 2012), 52.
8. Chip Heath and Dan Heath *Made to Stick: Why Some Ideas Survive and Others Die* (New York: Random House, 2007).
9. Tiffany A. Ito, Jeff T. Larsen, N. Kyle Smith, and John T. Cacioppo, "Negative Information Weighs More Heavily on the Brain: The Negativity Bias in Evaluative Categorizations," *Journal of Personality and Social Psychology* 75, no. 4 (1998): 887–900.

Chapter 2

1. Alvin Toffler, *Future Shock* (New York: Random House, 1970).
2. Richard H. Thaler and Cass R. Sunstein, "Libertarian Paternalism," *American Economic Review* 93 (2003): 175–199.
3. Jennifer S. Lerner, Ye Li, Piercarlo Valdesolo, and Karim S. Kassam, "Emotions and Decision Making," *Annual Review of Psychology* 66 (2015): 799–823.
4. Karla Gutierrez, "10 Compelling Reasons You Should Use Templates for eLearning," 2012, http://info.shiftelearning.com/blog/bid/214586/10-Compelling-Reasons-You-Should-Use-Templates-for-eLearning.
5. Stewart I. Donaldson, *The Future of Evaluation in Society: A Tribute to Michael Scriven* (Charlotte, NC: Information Age Publishing, 2013).
6. Antonio Damasio, *Descartes' Error: Emotion, Reason, and the Human Brain* (New York: Putnam, 1994).
7. Ibid., 245.
8. Dan Boudreau, "Creating the Ideal Learning Environment: Emotional," trainerhub.com, 2012, http://trainerhub.com/creating-the-ideal-learning-environment-emotional/; Dan Boudreau, "Creating The Ideal Learning Environment: Physical," trainerhub.com, 2013, http://trainerhub.com/creating-the-ideal-learning-environment-physical/.
9. Kevin Daum, "5 Ways to Overcome the Naysayers," *Inc.*, August 23, 2013, http://www.inc.com/kevin-daum/5-ways-to-overcome-the-naysayers.html.
10. Victor Lipman, "'Don't Let Perfect Be the Enemy of Good'; Tips to Help Tame Perfectionism," *Forbes*, March 13, 2014, http://www.forbes.com/sites/victorlipman/2014/03/13/dont-let-perfect-be-the-enemy-of-good-tips-to-help-tame-perfectionism/#635860bd74ce.
11. Joseph Straubhaar, Robert LaRose, and Lucinda Davenport, *Media Now: Understanding Media, Culture, and Technology*, 9th ed. (Belmont, CA: Wadsworth Publishing, 2016).
12. Chip Heath and Dan Heath, *Decisive: How to Make Better Choices in Life and Work.* (New York: Crown Business, 2013).
13. William H. Whyte, Jr., "Groupthink," *Fortune,* March 1952, pp. 114–117.

Chapter 3

1. Charles Duhigg, *The Power of Habit: Why We Do What We Do in Life and Business* (New York: Random House, 2014).
2. Ibid.
3. Merriam-Webster online, http://www.merriam-webster.com/dictionary/culture.
4. Charles Duhigg, *The Power of Habit.*
5. Mick Healey, "Linking Research and Teaching: Exploring Disciplinary Spaces and the Role of Inquiry-Based Learning," in *Reshaping the University: New Relationships between Research, Scholarship and Teaching,* ed. R. Barnett (New York: McGraw-Hill, 2005), 67–78.

Chapter 4

1. Brad Phillips, "Improving Response Time in Education," blog post, Michael & Susan Dell Foundation, May 12, 2015, 2015. https://www.msdf.org/blog/2015/05/brad-phillips-improving-response-time-in-education/.
2. "What Are Leading, Lagging and Coincident Indicators? What Are They For?" *Investopedia,* 2012, http://www.investopedia.com/ask/answers/177.asp.
3. Moira Reilly, "How and Why to Set Leading Indicators," November 5, 2015, https://www.clearpointstrategy.com/set-leading-indicators/.
4. AFT Higher Education, *Student Persistence in College: More Than Counting Caps and Gowns* (Washington, DC: American Federation of Teachers, 2003).

Chapter 5

1. Community College Research Center. (http://ccrc.tc.columbia.edu/).
2. Center for Community College Student Engagement. (http://www.ccsse.org/center/).
3. Achieving the Dream. (http://achievingthedream.org/resources/achieving-the-dream-interventions-showcase).
4. Merriam-Webster online, http://www.merriam-webster.com/dictionary/criteria.
5. Josipa Roksa and Juan Carlos Calcagno, "Catching Up in Community Colleges: Academic Preparation and Transfer to Four-Year Institutions," *Teachers College Record* 112, no. 1 (2010): 260–288.
6. Lee M. Upcraft and John N. Gardner, *The Freshman Year Experience: Helping Students Survive and Succeed in College* (San Francisco: Jossey-Bass, 1989).
7. John T. Cacioppo and William Patrick, *Loneliness: Human Nature and the Need for Social Connection* (New York: W.W. Norton, 2008).

8. Jordan E. Horowitz, Brad C. Phillips, and John Yopp, "Tuning in Community Colleges: A Study of the Development and Uses of Student Learning Outcomes," *Journal of Applied Research in the Community Colleges* 23, no. 1 (Spring 2016): 17–26.

9. Kay McClenney, *A Matter of Degrees: Engaging Practices, Engaging Students.* (Austin, TX: Center for Community College Student Engagement, 2013).

10. Ibid.

11. Gloria Ladson-Billings, "Toward a Theory of Culturally Relevant Pedagogy," *American Educational Research Journal* 32, no. 3 (June 2016): 465–491.

12. Kay McClenney, personal communication, 2005.

13. Thomas Bailey, Shanna Smith Jaggars, and Davis Jenkins, *Redesigning America's Community Colleges: A Clearer Path to Success* (Cambridge, MA: Harvard University Press, 2015).

14. Marilyn Ann Louise Hamilton, *Mathematics Boot Camps: A Strategy for Helping Students to Bypass Remedial Courses* (Minneapolis, MN: Walden University, 2015).

15. Thad Nodine, Mina Dadgar, Andrea Venezia, and Kathy Reeves Bracco, *Acceleration in Developmental Education* (San Francisco: WestEd, 2013).

16. Ibid.

17. Rob Johnstone, *Guided Pathways Demystified: Exploring Ten Commonly Asked Questions* About Implementing Pathways, National Center for Inquiry & Improvement (NCII), http://www.inquiry2improvement.com/publications-resources.

18. Bailey, Jaggars, and Jenkins, *Redesigning America's Community Colleges.*

19. Alberto Cabrera et al., *The Role of Mentoring in College Access and Success.* (Washington, DC: Institute for Higher Education Policy, 2011).

20. John P. Kotter, *Accelerate: Building Strategic Agility for a Faster-Moving World* (Boston: Harvard Business Review Press, 2014).

Chapter 6

1. K. J. Conrad and C. Roberts-Gray, *Evaluating Program Environments. New Directions for Program Evaluation*, 40th ed. (San Francisco: Jossey-Bass, 1988).

2. Stewart I. Donaldson, *The Future of Evaluation in Society: A Tribute to Michael Scriven* (Charlotte, NC: Information Age Publishing, 2013).

3. Bobbi Bilnoski. *RASIC: Roles, Accountability, and Responsibility Matrix*, https://4good.org/bobbi-bilnoski/r-a-s-i-c-roles-accountability-and-responsibility-matrix.

Chapter 7

1. Long Beach City College, *College Facts, 2016*, accessed November 6, 2016, http://www.lbcc.edu/PresidentsOffice/documents/08-31-16_Collegefacts.pdf.

2. Pacific Gateway, *Pacific Gateway Workforce Investment Network (PGWIN): Economic and Demographic Analysis*, paper presented to the Workforce Investment Board, accessed November 7, 2016, http://www.pacific-gateway .org/c17/small-pacific_gateway-workforce-investment_report_02-12-16% 20(2).pdf.

3. Long Beach City College, *College Facts, 2016*.

4. Percentages provided by the Long Beach City College Office of Institutional Effectiveness, November 6, 2016.

5. Office of Institutional Effectiveness, Long Beach City College *Do Long Beach City College Students Have Housing Needs?* (Long Beach, CA: Long Beach City College, December 3, 2015), Retrieved on March 31, 2017, at http:// www.lbcc.edu/IE/documents/ResearchBriefs/Housing-Needs-Survey-Fall 2016.pdf.

6. Long Beach City College, *College Facts, 2016*.

7. "LBCC Degrees and Certificates List," accessed November 7, 2016, http:// www.lbcc.edu/Catalog/documents/Degree%20and%20Certs.pdf.

8. Office of Institutional Effectiveness, Long Beach City College, *Basic Skills Innovations at Long Beach City College* (Long Beach, CA: Long Beach City College, December 3, 2015), accessed March 31, 2017, http://www.lbcc .edu/IE/documents/ResearchBriefs/BasicSkills-Draft-7-2-1617.pdf.

9. "Renewed College Promise Memorandum of Understanding, 2014," accessed November 6, 2016, http://www.longbeachCollegepromise.org/ wp-content/uploads/2014/10/Signed-LB-Col-Promise-Pledge-2014.pdf.

10. *Long Beach College Promise Governor's Innovation Award Newsletter*, September 2016, http://www.lbcc.edu/Communications/documents/LBCP-Governor's%20Innovation%20Award_Newsletter_September%202016% 20.pdf.

11. "Be the Change" preconference to College Day website, accessed November 6, 2016, http://www.lbcc.edu/Collegeday/conference.cfm.

12. Thomas Bailey, Shanna Smith Jaggars, and Davis Jenkins, *Redesigning America's Community Colleges: A Clearer Path to Success* (Cambridge, MA: Harvard University Press, 2015).

13. *Long Beach City College 2016–2022 Strategic Plan for Transformational Improvement*, http://www.lbcc.edu/IE/Documents/StrategicPlan/LBCC-2016-2022-Strategic-Plan.pdf.

14. http://completionbydesign.org/sites/default/files/site-uploads/main-site/ pdf/loss_and_momentum_framework_rev_2013-04_0.pdf.

15. Cole Nussbaumer Knaflic, *Storytelling with Data: A Data Visualization Guide for Business Professionals* (Hoboken, NJ: John Wiley & Sons, Inc., 2015)

16. Preconference session, American Association of Community Colleges conference, Chicago, April 9, 2016.

17. Ibid.

18. Joseph Yeado, Kati Haycock, Rob Johnstone, and Priyadarshini Chaplot, *Learning from High-Performing and Fast-Gaining Institutions*, The Education Trust, January 2014, accessed November 7, 2016, http://postsecondary .gatesfoundation.org/wp-content/uploads/2014/09/The-Education-Trust _Higher-Education-Practice-Guide.pdf.

Chapter 8

1. California Community College Chancellors Office, *Student Equity Planning Fact Sheet* (Sacramento, CA: CCCCO, 2014).

2. Southwestern Community College District, *Fact Book 2015–2016* (Chula Vista, CA: Office of Institutional Research, Planning & Grants, 2017).

Chapter 9

1. Donald S. Wood and Gregory Williams, "Data-Driven Factors That Increase Student Course Completion: A Two-Year Study," in *Proceedings of the 9th National Symposium on Student Retention*, ed. Sandra Whalen (Norman, OK: University of Oklahoma, 2013), 142–152.

2. Texas Higher Education Coordinating Board and Permian Basin Workforce Development Board, txhighereddata.org.

ACKNOWLEDGMENTS

We live in a time of great opportunity and challenge for America's community colleges. We wrote this book with students in mind, confident that talented and dedicated educators can make better use of data to improve their decisions about how best to help students succeed and achieve their goals.

We thank our colleagues at the Institute for Evidence-Based Change for their support, suggestions, and help in preparing the manuscript; and our board for supporting the work.

This book would not be possible without the support of our spouses, Jackie Phillips and David Alexander.

Our colleagues Kay and Byron McClenney, Davis Jenkins, Naida Tushnet, and others too numerous to name helped guide our thinking. Thank you Michael Cowan, whose work on supporting decision making in the military helped us to begin this journey.

Thanks also to our contributors, Lauren Davis Sosenko, Angelica Suarez, Gregory Williams, and Donald Wood, who put our model into practice and took the time to write about their experiences.

Finally, we want to thank the great team at Harvard Education Press, especially Nancy Walser, who kept us moving forward, and editrix Monica Jainschigg.

ABOUT THE AUTHORS

Brad C. Phillips is President and CEO of the Institute for Evidence-Based Change (IEBC), where he leads the organization's focus on improving educational practice and outcomes in schools, colleges, and universities.

Over the last twenty years, Phillips has pioneered the collaborative collection and sharing of data across educational segments, focusing on helping educators use data to make classroom and institutional changes that improve student success. His IEBC work ranges from the grassroots to national education associations and includes state higher education systems, national organizations, foundations, and professional associations as well as local and regional educational institutions.

Phillips served for a number of years as a community college educator, researcher, and program director and founded the California Partnership for Achieving Student Success (Cal-PASS). He serves as a data facilitator for Achieving the Dream, a member of the Advisory Board of the Texas Student Success Center, and Ambassador with the Leap of Reason national initiative.

A frequent keynote speaker, Phillips also has authored numerous articles on education issues. His work has been published in *Education Week, Forbes, Good* magazine, *Community College Journal, New Directions for Community Colleges, Journal of Applied Research in the Community Colleges, American Educator, AACJC, Huffington Post, Medium,* and *Data Bus.*

He is the recipient of recognitions and honors for his innovative research and commitment to faculty involvement and student progress, including the Mertes Award for Excellence in Community College Research.

Phillips holds a bachelor's degree in psychology from California State University, Northridge, and a master's degree in psychology from California State University, Los Angeles. Before pursuing his doctoral degree, he worked as a therapist in community mental health. He earned his doctorate in psychology with an emphasis in research methods and statistics from Claremont Graduate University.

Jordan E. Horowitz is Vice President at the Institute for Evidence-Based Change. He joined the organization in 2007. He has extensive experience in improving data use at educational institutions, educational partnerships, and comprehensive school reform. Before joining IEBC, he was Senior Project Director in Evaluation Research at WestEd, where he directed the evaluations of numerous local, state, and federal programs. Horowitz also worked as a psychotherapist in public and private practice.

Horowitz is responsible for developing and managing IEBC projects funded by private foundations and public sources, including: improving data use in California's Linked Learning Initiative school districts; a review of Idaho's Educational Technology and Data Systems in Support of Students' College and Career Readiness; a national study linking postsecondary student and organizational data to inform the development of metrics for colleges and universities; and linking California's educational and social service data systems to identify outcomes for foster youth in California; among others. He provides professional development and technical assistance to improve the use of data in educational institutions and among stakeholders.

Most recently, Horowitz authored two pieces for the online journal *Medium* that encourage philanthropy to adopt a more data-informed approach to giving: *Getting Evaluations Right* and *Hack This!* He also co-edited the January 2014 volume of *New Directions for Community Colleges*, which explored the nation's college completion agenda, and coauthored a chapter about *Data Use and the College Completion Agenda* for the volume. He authored the book *Inside High School Reform: Making the Changes That Matter*. Other publications include *Partnering for Successful School Reform, College Ready by Design*, and *The New Alignment: High School Exit Expectations and College Entrance Expectations*.

Horowitz holds a BS in human development and public policy from Northwestern University and a MS in counseling psychology from the same institution. He also received a MA in applied social psychology from The Claremont Graduate School.

ABOUT THE CONTRIBUTORS

Lauren Davis Sosenko serves as the Director of Institutional Research at Long Beach City College, a Southern California community college enrolling over thirty thousand students each year. In this role, Sosenko manages the college's research projects and coaches faculty and staff to use data for improvement and increased student success. Before joining the college, Sosenko conducted program evaluations and consultant services for colleges and schools across the country for over thirteen years, first as a research associate at WestEd, and then as the Associate Director for Special Projects with the Institute for Evidence-Based Change.

Angelica Suarez has been an educational leader for over twenty years. She is committed to the transformational power of the community colleges. Suarez serves as the Vice President for Student Affairs for the Southwestern Community College District in Chula Vista, California. In this role, she provides the leadership for the district's student support services and programs, which serve approximately twenty thousand students each semester in five locations. Suarez is the past president of the California Community Colleges Chief Student Services Officers Administrators Association.

Gregory D. Williams is the president of Odessa College, where he began his journey in higher education as a student in 1983. Since Williams's return to Odessa in January 2007, the college has gone through a systematic transformation. Under his guidance, Odessa College was recently named a top-10 finalist for the 2017 Aspen Award, a distinction given to the top-performing community colleges in the nation and awarded the 2017 Rising Star Aspen Award.

Don Wood is Odessa College's first Vice President for Institutional Effectiveness. At Odessa, he has helped lead the college into a new era of data-informed decision making and provided scientific support and insight for several of the college's award winning programs. He started his community college experience as a faculty member at Odessa from a desire to give back to others what he had received through his education. Trained as a research scientist, Wood participated in discoveries of the genetics underlying several neuromuscular diseases and later, as an entrepreneur, helped start three medical development and service companies.

INDEX

accreditation reports, 89
Achieving the Dream (AtD), 100
　　Data Discovery Guide, 4
　　Interventions Showcase, 91
　　Leader College status, 154
　　leadership and data coaches, 4
　　Odessa College (OC), 154
actionable data, 8–9
activities instead of indicators, 74
adequately resourced interventions, 94
administrators improving student
　　success, 21
Advancement Via Individual
　　Determination. *See* AVID
　　(Advancement Via Individual
　　Determination)
American Association of Colleges and
　　Universities, 83
　　guided pathways, 129
analytic tools solving data use
　　problem, 56–57
Aspen Prize Rising Star Award (2017),
　　152, 154
assessment
　　baseline for interventions and
　　　outcomes, 112
　　habits, 67
　　lagging indicators, 111
　　leading indicators, 111
associate degrees for transfer (ADTs),
　　124–125
AtD. *See* Achieving the Dream (AtD)
AVID (Advancement Via Individual
　　Determination), 162–163
awareness, 113

basic skills for course success, 101–103
Basic Skills Initiative (BSI), 140
behavior
　　changing with data, 18
　　habits, 51
behavioral economics, 11
Be the Change plan
　　blueprint for stakeholders, 127
　　changing student experience, 131
　　Completion, 127
　　Connection, 127
　　data use, 127
　　Entry, 127
　　goals, 126
　　lagging indicators, 127, 128
　　leading indicators, 127, 128
　　Long Beach City College, 131
　　metrics, 126–127, 129–130
　　Progress, 127, 131
　　stakeholders review of data, 130–131
　　target setting, 130–132
　　Transition, 127
　　understanding meaning of data,
　　　131
big goals, 72
Bill and Melinda Gates Foundation,
　　83
Boudreau, Dan, 41
BSI. *See* Basic Skills Initiative (BSI)
buildup-breakdown principle, 31

California Acceleration project, 102
California Community College Board
　　of Governors, 138

California Community Colleges Chancellor's Office (CCCCO) Student Success Task Force (SSTF), 137–139

California Community College Scorecard, 129

California Partnership for Achieving Student Success (Cal-PASS), 22

California State University partnering with Long Beach City College (LBCC), 125

CBD. *See* Completion by Design (CBD)

CCRC. *See* Community College Research Center (CCRC)

Center for Community College Student Engagement, 91, 146

Center for Student Engagement, 98

change, 104–105

change management strategy, 104

Chapman, Marsha, 17–18

charts, reducing information on, 37–38

choice architecture, 38–39

Civitas, 128

classroom attendance, 159

classroom interventions, 94

coalition of leaders, 104

college completion, 103

combination relationships between leading indicators, 79

Community College Research Center (CCRC), 91, 100, 146

Redesigning Community College, 126

community colleges
course retention, 97–98
culture, 169
data, 2–3, 6, 7, 53–56
decision-making process, 21–22
dropout rate, 156–157
faculty and staff, 19–20
feeder high schools partnerships, 96
first-year experience (FYE) program, 87–88, 100
funding, 4, 138, 175
habits, 51–56, 58–59
institutional culture, 53

lack of focus, 175–176
late enrollment, 98
leadership changes, 176
leading and lagging indicators, 11
measuring student progress, 129
never letting a good crisis go to waste, 58
overcoming resistance, 104–105
participation rates, 89–90
recruitment efforts, 89–90
resistance to change, 176–177
strategic planning, 89
student success and completion, 137–139
students unprepared for college experience, 95–96
student support services, 138
unaddressed challenges, 20–21
undergraduate students, 3
underlying assumptions about population, 31

Completion by Design (CBD)
funding, 4
key performance indicators (KPI), 4–5
metrics, 4–5
Understanding the Student Experience Framework initiative, 126

completion outcomes, 155

completion signaling systems, 103

compliance, necessary data for, 27

confirmation bias, 45–46

consensus, 47–48

consequences, 40

context, 40

continuous improvement
assessment, 111–112
how and where to correct, 119–120
implementation, 115–118
monitoring progress, 118–120
planning, 113–115

corequisite remediation, 103

course
acceleration, 102
completion, 98–99

retention, 90–91, 97–98
  success, 90–91
credit attainment, 90
criteria, 93
  moving to interventions, 94–95
criteria-setting approach, 93–95
cultural competence training, 99

Damasio, Antonio, 41
data, 2–3
  accessing, 56–57
  accuracy, 22–26, 30
  Achieving the Dream (AtD), 4
  actionable, 8–9
  administrators, faculty, and staff use
    of, 17–18
  behavior, 18
  buildup-breakdown principle, 31
  celebrating use of, 64
  clear categories of, 30
  collecting and acting on, 4, 23
  comparison information, 30–31
  Completion by Design (CBD), 4–5
  compliance, 27
  connecting emotionally and
    cognitively with, 39
  consensus, 47–48
  context, 62
  current efforts to use, 4–5
  data entry, 22–24
  decision making, 3–4, 27
  directing reader, 28–29
  disaggregating, 82–83, 174–175
  displaying, 9, 37–38
  educators, 3
  effective use of, 6
  embracing use of, 55–56
  engaging with, 48, 63
  experts, 57
  Field of Dreams approach, 18
  focusing on, 6–7, 26, 30
  format of, 56
  framing, 60, 62
  good data, 56

habits, 51–68, 59–64
headlines, 27–29
helpful, 24
hoped-for reaction to, 62
improving use of, 3
increasing use of, 173–174
indicators, 57, 63, 88–89
information overload, 36–38
Information Systems (IS) office, 5
Institutional Research (IR) office, 5
judgment and, 36
keeping simple, 47, 62–63
making it real, 63
making sense of, 36
maximizing understanding of, 174
meetings, 47–48, 59–64
missing, 31–32
models, 53–56
National Benchmarking Project
  (NBP), 5
noise, 63
not appreciating, 54–55
obstacles to strategic use of, 7–9
planning and, 54
positive or negative, 60
problem solving with, 18
quality of, 23–24
questions to ask about, 29–30
reaction to, 43, 47
reporting, 24–26, 32
reports, 37
in service of equity, 137–149
stakeholder engagement, 123–135
state accountability systems, 5
story about, 39–40, 47–48
student information system (SIS), 7
study everything approach, 18
technology and, 56
template for conversations about,
  29–33
too much, 56
unavailable, 80
Voluntary Framework of
  Accountability (VFA), 5
data analytics, 6–7, 10–11

assumptions, 19–22
educators, 17–33
efforts in, 9
faculty and staff, 19–20
negative data, 19–20
problems, 20–21
useful, useable, and actionable, 9
data champions, 59
Model 1 colleges, 64
Model 2 colleges, 65
Data Discovery Guide, 4
data-driven reform, 12
data entry, 22–24
data jockey approach, 8
data use habits, 53–54
data use model, 9, 10–12
data use paradigm
challenges, 175–177
data use, 173–174
disaggregating data, 174–175
educators, 174
funding, 175
lack of focus, 175–176
lagging indicators, 174
leadership, 176
leading indicators, 174
metrics, 174
resistance to change, 176–177
data use problem, 56–57
Daum, Kevin, 43
decision making, 22
consensus in meetings, 63
data, 27
emotions and, 41–45
Long Beach City College (LBCC), 123
Model 3 colleges, 66
positive environment, 41–45
decision-making problems
confirmation bias, 45–46
narrow focus, 45
overconfidence, 46–47
short-term emotion, 46
dependent variables (DV), 86
Descartes' Error (Damasio), 41
dictionary.com, 19

disaggregating data, 82–83, 174–175
dropout rate, 156–157
Drop Rate Improvement Program,
156–160, 164, 167, 169–170
clear expectations, 158
first-time-in-college (FTIC) students,
159
increasing students grades, 158
interacting with students, 157
meeting with students early in
semester, 157–158
monitoring student behavior, 157
socioeconomically disadvantaged (Pell
grant-supported) students, 159
student behavior transformation, 159
student success rates, 159
Duhigg, Charles, 11, 52

early warning systems, 98–99
educators
asking questions, 64–65
change management strategy, 104
changing students' lives, 174
data, 3, 19–20, 54–55
data analytics, 17–33
decision making, 4
denial of data, 20
poor performance of students, 31
stages of grief, 19–20
Einstein, Albert, 101
emotion blinding us to options, 46
equitable outcomes, 155
equity between student groups, 112
evaluation and habits, 67
evidence-based decision making
institutionalizing, 161–165
Odessa College (OC), 154–155, 160,
165

faculty
professional development, 97, 99
reviewing data, 65
student performance, 19–20

student success improvements, 21
feeder high schools partnership with
    community colleges, 96
Field of Dreams approach, 18
figures, reducing information in, 37–38
first-time-in-college (FTIC) students, 81
    Drop Rate Improvement Program, 159
    first-year experience (FYE) program,
        87–88
    mentoring programs, 101
    role models, 100
first-year experience (FYE) program,
    65–66, 96, 100
    first-time-in-college (FTIC) students,
        87–88
formative assessments, 109–110
framing theory, 44–45
FTIC students. *See* first-time-in-college
    (FTIC) students
Future Shock (Toffler), 37
FYE program. *See* first-year experience
    (FYE) program

GANTT charts, 115, 116
gatekeeper courses, 90
Georgia State University, 129
goals
    identifying, 89
    misidentifying as indicators, 75
good data use in meetings template
    agenda, 61
    clarity of purpose, 61–62
    consensus on decision, 63
    data and discussions, 62–63
    framing positive or negative data, 60
    identifying issue, 61–62
    introducing data, 61–62
    keeping it simple, 62–63
    making it real, 63
    before meeting, 60–61
    participants, 62–63
    priming, 60
    safety and familiarity, 61
    setting context, 62

graduation rates, 90
groupthink, 47–48
guided pathways, 100, 103, 129
guide to developing indicators, 80–83

habit change, 58–59
habit-changing strategies
    Model 1 colleges, 64–65
    Model 2 colleges, 65–66
    Model 3 colleges, 66
habit loop, 52–53, 59
habits, 51
    assessment, 67
    data use, 53–54
    evaluation, 67
    meetings, 59–64
    models for data, 53–56
    Pepsodent toothpaste story, 52–53
halo effect, 61
headlines and data usefulness, 27–29
Heath, Chip, 45
Heath, Dan, 45
Hopkins, Claude, 52, 53
HSI Title V Grant, 140

IEBC
    data use model, 126, 128
    facilitator to develop student equity
        plan, 142
IEPI. *See* Institutional Effectiveness
    Partnership Initiative (IEPI)
implementation
    continuous improvement, 115–118
    planning monitoring, 113–114
    RASIC (Responsible, Approves,
        Supports, Informed, Consulted)
        tool, 115–118
independent leading indicators, 78–79
independent variables (IV), 86
indicators, 63
    activities instead of, 74
    course retention, 90–91, 97–98
    course success, 90–91

indicators, *continued*
  credit attainment, 90
  defining, 74–75
  equity between student groups, 112
  first course students take, 90
  goals misidentified as, 75
  graduation rates, 90
  guide to developing, 80–83
  interventions, 87–106
  items not indicators, 74
  lagging indicators, 71–85
  leading indicators, 71–85
  looking inward, 89–91
  Model 3 colleges, 66
  persistence rates, 90
  perspective, 75–76
  progress metrics, 90
  recruitment efforts, 89–90
  selecting, 80, 88–89
  skill level of entering students, 90
  student achievement, 112
  student engagement, 112
  student success, 91–93
  targets not being met, 119
  who college is serving, 112
information, 9
  choice architecture, 38–39
  food and, 43
  positive before negative, 31
  presenting, 44–45
  threats from negative, 19
information overload, 36–38
information systems (IS) offices, 5
information technology (IT) offices, 114
institutional culture, 53
Institutional Effectiveness Partnership
    Initiative (IEPI), 5
Institutional Research (IR) office, 5, 8
Intent to Complete cohort, 134–135
interventions
  adequately resourced, 94
  aligning to indicators of success,
    87–106
  baseline for, 112
  basic skills course success, 101–103

basic skills sequence success, 102
choosing wrong, 88
classroom, 94
college completion, 103
course acceleration, 102
course completion, 98–99
criteria-setting approach, 93–95
doable, 94
first-year experience (FYE) program,
    100
guided pathways, 100
impact on population, 88, 93
implementing at scale, 93
judgments, 118
mentoring programs, 101
monitoring, 107–120
moving from criteria to, 94–95
not going as planned, 119–120
persistence, 100–101
policies and practices, 91–93
problem focus, 89–91
professional development, 97
qualitative data, 119
refresher summer boot camps,
    101–102
research-based, 93
So what? question, 88–89
student service interventions, 94
student success, 91–93, 95–104
students understanding relevance of
    learning, 97–98
systemic effect, 94
Interventions Showcase, 91
Investopedia, 72
IR office. *See* Institutional Research (IR)
    office
issue of the week problem, 175
IT offices. *See* information technology
    (IT) offices

Jenkins, Davis, 129
Johnstone, Rob, 102, 129
judgment
  data, 36

effect of emotion on, 41
fostering by telling story, 39–40
interventions, 118
policies, 118
supports, 118

key performance indicators (KPI), 57
Knaflic, Cole Nussbaumer, 128
Kotter, John, 104–105
KPI. *See* key performance indicators
(KPI), 57
Kübler-Ross, Elizabeth, 19

labor-market outcomes, 155
lagging indicators, 71–85
    accreditation and state
        accountability reports, 89
    assessment, 111
    backward mapping to leading
        indicators, 81–82
    benchmark, 73
    Be the Change plan, 127, 128
    big goals, 72
    common, 83, 84
    data use paradigm, 174
    defining, 82
    degree attainment, 78
    dependent variables (DV), 86
    independent leading indicators
        leading to, 78–79
    indicators influencing, 81
    influencing outcomes, 72–73
    leading indicators, 73, 76–80
    not actionable, 72
    Odessa College, 151–171
    perspective, 75–76
    student equity committee, 145
late registration policy, 98
LBCC. *See* Long Beach City College
    (LBCC)
leadership
    changing, 176
    not valuing data, 54

leading indicators, 71–85
    actionable, 73, 77
    assessment, 111, 119
    Be the Change plan, 127, 128
    classroom attendance, 159
    combination relationships between, 79
    common, 83, 84
    data use paradigm, 174
    defining, 82
    independent, 78–79
    independent variables (IV), 86
    lagging indicators, 73, 76–82
    metrics, 73
    Odessa College, 151–171
    perspective complicating, 75–76
    sequential, 76–77
    status of, 112
    student equity committee, 145
    student progress, 73
    students not achieving, 77
    window of opportunity to act, 73
learning outcomes, 155
Long Beach City College (LBCC), 12,
    177
    acceleration and technological
        products, 125
    aligning success measures to
        strategic plan, 128
    alignment of college measures in all
        plans, 134
    associate degrees for transfer (ADTs),
        124–125
    basic skills, 125
    Be the Change plan, 126–130
    Civitas, 128
    completion rate, 126
    connecting stakeholders to strategic
        plan, 128
    Connection metrics, 130
    data reports, 128
    decision making and improvement,
        123
    degrees and certificates, 124–125
    engaging stakeholders with data,
        123–135

Long Beach City College, *continued*
  evidence-driven, 123
  faculty and staff, 125–126, 128
  financial need of students, 124
  first-generation college-going
    students, 124
  Governor's Innovation Award, 125
  guided pathways, 129
  history of, 124
  IEBC data use model, 126, 128
  improvement processes, 132–133
  industries around, 124
  Intent to Complete cohort, 129–130,
    134–135
  key stakeholders, 134
  Liberal Arts Campus (LAC), 124
  measuring success, 134
  meetings, 134
  metrics impacting work of, 134–135
  multiple measures placement, 123
  Office of Institutional Effectiveness
    (IE), 123, 126
  Pacific Coast Campus, 124
  partnering with Long Beach Unified
    School District and California
    State University, 125
  perspective, 132–133
  Progress metrics, 130
  strategic plan, 126–130
  Strategic Plan Oversight Dashboard,
    133
  Strategic Plan Oversight Taskforce
    (SPOT), 126–128
  Student Success Scorecard, 132
  Tableau technology, 128
  target setting, 130–132
  tracking sophomore standing, 130
Long Beach Unified School District
  partnering with Long Beach City
    College (LBCC), 125
Lumley, Tris, 18

Mathway, 102
McClenney, Kay, 99

meetings
  agenda, 61
  arrangements for, 61
  breaks, 42
  clarifying expected outcomes, 47, 62
  clarity of purpose, 61
  consensus, 47–48, 63
  environmental factors, 42
  framing data, 60
  good data use, 59–64
  groupthink, 47–48
  hoped-for reaction, 62
  identifying issue to be addressed, 47,
    61–62
  introducing data, 47–48, 61–63
  keeping it simple, 62–63
  making it real, 63
  participants, 47, 60–62
  postmortems, 48–49
  priming, 60
  setting context, 47, 62
mentoring programs, 101, 103
Merriam-Webster Dictionary, 53, 93
meta-majors, 100, 103
metrics and data use paradigm, 174
missing data, 31–32
Model 1 colleges, 54–55, 64–65
Model 2 colleges, 54, 65–66
Model 3 colleges, 55–56, 66
monitoring interventions
  formative assessments, 109–110
  outcome, 109
  process, 108–109
  program structure, 108
  qualitative data, 110
  quantitative data, 110
  summative assessments, 109–110
monitoring progress of continuous
  improvement, 118–120

narrow focus, 45
National Benchmarking Project (NBP), 5
NBP. *See* National Benchmarking
  Project (NBP)

negative data, 60
never letting a good crisis go to waste, 58
new shiny penny mentality, 175
noise, 63
numbers
  putting a face on, 40
  turning into faces, 47–48
  turning percentages into, 40

obstacles to strategic use of data, 8–9
Odessa College (OC), 178
  Achieving the Dream (AtD), 154
  areas in need of improvement,
    164–165
  Aspen Prize Rising Star Award
    (2017), 152, 154
  AVID (Advancement Via Individual
    Determination), 162–163
  Birthday Bashes, 168
  board of trustees, 153
  classroom attendance, 159
  Coffee and Conversations, 160, 168
  communications between
    stakeholders, 167–168
  completion outcomes, 155
  continuous growth, 162
  Dean of Teaching and Learning, 165
  defunding by Texas legislature, 152,
    153, 156
  doing more to help students, 155–
    156
  dropout rate, 156–157
  Drop Rate Improvement Program,
    156–160, 164, 167, 169–170
  eight-week terms, 162
  employees, 166–170
  enrollment, 151, 153, 155–156,
    161–162
  evidence-based decision making,
    154–155, 160–165
  failing facilities, 153
  history of, 152–153
  in-class retention, 155–156
  initiatives, 161
  instruction, 156
  labor-market outcomes, 155
  lagging indicators, 151–171
  Leader College status, 154
  leading indicators, 151–171
  learning outcomes, 155
  meeting weekly, 161–162, 168
  OC All-In program, 168–169
  online courses, 166
  standards of excellence, 170
  strategic planning, 161–162
  Strategies for Success course, 162–163
  student dropout rates, 164
  student-focused programs, 161–162
  student outcomes, 153–156, 165, 169
  student services, 156
  student success, 151–152, 161, 167,
    170
  Student Success Coach program, 164
  Vice President for Institutional
    Effectiveness, 161
Odessa Community College, 12
On Death and Dying (Kübler-Ross), 19
organizational habits for effective use
  of data, 51–68
organizations changing practices and
  policies, 21–22
outcome, 109
overconfidence, 46–47

participation rates, 89–90
pathways of study, 100, 103
Pepsodent Company, 52
Pepsodent toothpaste story and habits,
  52–53
percentages, turning into numbers, 40
persistence, 90, 100–101
perspective complicating indicators,
  75–76
planning
  awareness, 113
  continuous improvement, 113–115
  data and, 54
  identifying goals from documents, 89

planning, *continued*
  information technology (IT) offices, 114
  institutional research (IR) offices, 114
  monitoring implementation, 113–114
  project meetings, 115
  tools, 115
policies
  judgments, 118
  organizations changing, 21–22
  reviewing, 120
  student success, 91–93
population, underlying assumptions about, 31
positive data, 60
positive decision making
  food and information, 43
  framing effects, 44–45
  priming, 43–44
  setting, 41–43
postmortems for meetings, 48–49
power-data users, 56
The Power of Habit (Duhigg), 52
practices
  changes in, 21–22
  student success, 91–93
priming, 60
priming theory, 43–44
problems, 40
  accreditation and state accountability reports, 89
  acknowledging and making change, 20–21
  assessment, 111–112
  beliefs about, 45–46
  fixing, 21
  focus, 45, 89–91
  planning documents, 89
  response to, 43
  solving themselves with data, 18
process, 108–109
professional development, 97, 99
program structure, 108
progress metrics, 90

project meetings, 115
Promise, 125

qualitative data, 110, 119
quantitative data, 110
Quantway, 102
questions to ask about data, 29–30

RASIC (Responsible, Approves, Supports, Informed, Consulted) tool, 116–118
recent organizational theory, 11
recruitment efforts, 89–90
recursive reports, 57
Redesigning America's Community Colleges, 100
refresher summer boot camps, 101–102
regression analyses, 86
relationships, 29
reports
  breaking into multiple documents, 37
  pattern for presenting information, 39
research-based interventions, 93
resistance to change, 176–177
resolution, 40

Scriven, Michael, 39, 109–110
sequence success, 102
sequential leading indicators, 76–77
Seymour-Campbell Student Success Act (2012), 138, 139
short-term emotion, 46
SIS. *See* student information system (SIS)
skill level of entering students, 90
SLOs. *See* student learning outcomes (SLOs)
socioeconomically disadvantaged (Pell grant-supported) students and Drop Rate Improvement Program, 159
Sosenko, Lauren Davis, 12, 177
South County Education Collaborative, 148

Southwestern College (SWC), 12, 177–178
  Academic Senate, 140
  context, 139–141
  data in service of equity, 137–149
  evaluating interventions, 147–148
  facilitator, 141–142
  legislative context, 137–139
  Office of Equity, Diversity and Inclusion (EDI), 147
  partnership with high school district, 148
  student equity committee, 140
  student equity plan, 140–149
  student population, 139–140
  student success and completion agenda, 140
  Vice President for Academic Affairs, 140
  Vice President for Student Affairs, 140
Southwestern Community College District (SCCD), 139
So what? question, 88–89
SPOT. *See* Strategic Plan Oversight Taskforce (SPOT)
SSSP. *See* Student Success and Support Program (SSSP)
staff
  reviewing data, 65
  student performance, 19–20
  student success, 21
stakeholders, engaging with data, 123–135
state accountability reports, 89
state accountability systems, 5
statistics and understanding relationships, 29
Statway, 102
stories fostering judgment, 39–40
Storytelling with Data (Knaflic), 128
strategic planning, 89
  Be the Change plan, 126
  Long Beach City College (LBCC), 126–130

Strategic Plan Oversight Taskforce (SPOT), 126, 127
  Being the Change, 132
  identifying stakeholders, 128
  metrics for measuring degree-applicable units, 129–130
Strategies for Success course, 162–163
student achievement, 112
student engagement, 112
student equity committee
  best practices, 146
  IEBC facilitator, 142
  interventions, 146–147
  lagging indicators, 145
  leading indicators, 145
  potential interventions, 145–146
  priming technique, 142
  reformatting data to aid understanding, 143–145
  role of, 142
  students completing basic skills curriculum, 143–145
  student success, 147
  World Café event, 144–145
student equity plan
  efforts metrics, 138–139
  facilitator, 141–142
  Southwestern College (SWC), 141–149
student information system (SIS), 7
student learning outcomes (SLOs), 96
students
  basic skills course success, 101–103
  course retention, 97–98
  early warning systems, 98–99
  entering students skill level, 90
  failing next course in sequence, 96
  first course taken by, 90
  leading indicators, 77
  learning outcomes for, 98
  performance, 19–20, 31, 82–83
  persistence, 100–101
  readiness to begin college-level work, 95–96
  relevance of what they learn, 97–98

students, *continued*
  wanting to feel cared about, 97
student-service interventions, 94
student success
  additional resources for, 95
  awareness, 113
  interventions, 95–104
  leading indicators, 119
  Odessa College, 151–152
  policies and practices aligned with,
    91–93
  preparedness, 95–96
Student Success and Support Program
  (SSSP), 140
Student Success Coach program, 164
Student Success Initiative, 138
Student Success Task Force (SSTF),
  137–139
study everything approach, 18, 22
Suarez, Angelica, 12, 177
successful course completion, 98–99
summative assessments, 109–110
supplemental instruction, 99

tables, 37–38
technology and format of data, 56
templates
  change over time, 39

for conversations about data, 29–33
guiding discussions, 48
habit of good data use, 59–64
increasing flexibility, 39
planning, 115
power of, 38–39
Toffler, Alvin, 36–37

undergraduate students, 3
*Understanding the Student Experience
  Framework* initiative, 126
US Department of Education
  data quality, 23
  Institute for Educational Sciences, 9

VFA. *See* Voluntary Framework of
  Accountability (VFA)
Voluntary Framework of
  Accountability (VFA), 5

who college is serving, 112
Williams, Gregory, 12, 153, 156, 167,
  178
Wood, Donald, 12, 156, 161, 178
World Café event, 144–145